Breville Smart Air Fryer Oven Cookbook 2021

***1000** Easy Tasty Yet Healthy Recipes Cooked by Breville Smart Air Fryer Toast Oven for Beginners and Advanced Users*

By Jenson Homolka

Table of Contents

Book Description

Oven, a kitchen utensil, is an amazing helper with great technology that outperforms traditional gas ovens. It is one of the most convenient and time-saving utensils that lock all the nutrients inside the food. However, we want to introduce to you the new Breville BOV900BSS Smart Oven. The new Breville BOV900BSS smart oven can not only perform as a regular oven but also as a perfect kitchen utensil for roasting, frying, and dehydrating food.

So, if you are a foodie, like cooking food, and are looking for a simple, affordable and best way to give yourself a variety of cooking experiences without burning the food, then the Breville BOV900BSS smart oven is for you.

As the title of the book indicates, our content includes the following aspects.

- Product Introduction
- Essential Equipment
- Useful Buttons and Functions
- Benefits of Using Breville Smart Air Fryer Toast Oven
- Tips and Cautions for Using Breville Smart Air Fryer Toast Oven
- Cooking schedule
- Conclusion

Along with this, we also added some pictures of home appliances so that the overall transaction can proceed smoothly. There is no doubt that the Breville BOV900BSS Smart Oven is a countertop utensil that can bring you various possibilities such as roasting, dehydrating, and air frying.

Introduction

The product price starts at only $399.95 and it is a multifunctional electrical utensil that dominates all other models in the category of toaster ovens. No matter what you pour in this oven, it will never disappoint you and only bring you mouthwatering results!

Since it is a countertop oven, it needs a large counter space to fit it in the kitchen. The rest features of the product ensure the customer the best results, which are promised by the device manufacturers.

This Breville smart oven impresses everyone with its 1800 watt of power with 2 –speed convection and about six independent heating elements.

On top of that, this utensil is quite powerful.

As the name suggests, different from a traditional oven where the reheated food still remains cold, it is a convection toaster oven that heats food all the ways up instead of just warming it up in the back of the oven.

Every time you put food in it, you can always expect to get delicious and crunchy food in return. It is a classic oven for baking, roasting, air frying, and hydrating. The temperature control feature is excellent and once you start making food with it, there is no need to you to buy an air fryer anymore.

SELECT
START | STOP
TEMP
TIME

Chapter 1: Essentials You Must Know

This smart oven is a multifunction device with magic effects. Just like its name suggests, it brings you greasy-free items in a short time. The Breville is equipped with about 13 functions that make it stand out from any other appliances.

It has an element called IQ, making it possible for it to be equipped with preset cooking modes and to allow users to set the fan speed and temperature. Therefore, if any recipe needs to be adjusted, users can easily set it. The settings of this oven are as follows.

1. Toast
2. Bake
3. Broil
4. Roast
5. Reheat
6. Air fry
7. Proof
8. Slow cook
9. Dehydrate
10. Cookies
11. Bagel
12. Broil
13. Pizza

However, for convection, you can switch to a higher fan. During the cooking process, the light switch can help you see the food inside.

Its LCD panel is very bright. Even if you are cooking in a dark room, it can support you with the cooking process without turning on the kitchen lights.

Below the LCD panel are four dials and a few small buttons. Therefore, users need to adjust the settings when using electrical appliances. Reading the manufacturer's manual is helpful in this regard. The number of things and recipes it can cook is far beyond imagination. From roasting turkey to baking brownies, it is much better than a wall oven.

Features

- 5-in-1 function with the facility of an air fryer, a dehydrator, and a microwave.
- Element IQ Cooking.
- Massive interior – it can easily fit 14-pounds of turkey, 22 muffin trays, and a lot more.
- Cleanup is easy because its non-stick coating makes the maintenance and cleaning process very easy.
- Four trays can be used at a time.
- Quick pre-heating and cooking functions are available.

- 2 Year Limited Product Warranty
- Power: 1800 Watts
- 2 speed convection fans

Simple but Useful Buttons and Functions

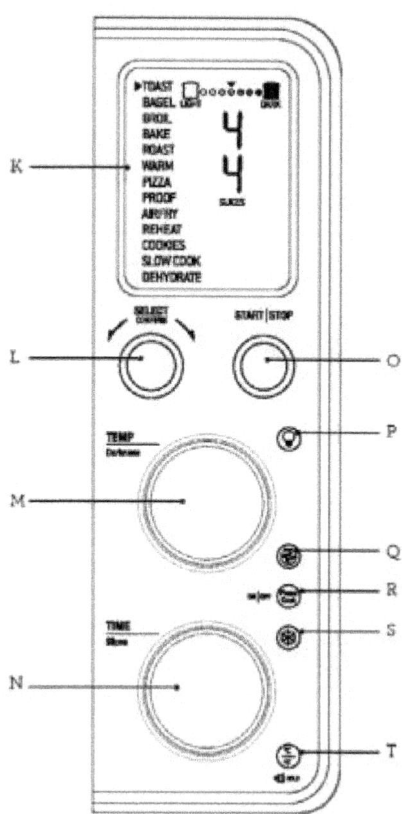

K=LCD Screen

L=Selector Confirm Dial (It Is A Rotate Remind Button)

M=Temperature Dial That Is Used to Control the Darkness for Toast and Bagel

N=Time Dial; It Is A Toast and Bagel Slice Section

O=Start and Stop Button That Turns Off and On the Cooking Process.

P=Oven Light Button That Helps to Peek Inside the Food

Q=Convection Button

R=Phase Cook Button

S=Frozen Food Button

T=volume adjustment and temperate conversion button

Oven Function Overview

Functions	Presets	Preheat	Range
Bake	325 Degrees F 30 Minutes Convection	Yes	>390 Degrees F For 4 Hours 300-390degrees F For 8 Hours 210-300 Degrees F For 12 Hours
Boil	High	No	Low. Med, High 20 Minutes
Bagel	Darkness 4 Slices 4	No	Darkness1-7 Slices1-10
Warm	160 Degrees F	No	>390 Degrees F For 4 Hours 300-390degrees F For 8 Hours 210-300 Degrees F For 12 Hours
Pizza	375 Degrees F 20 Minutes	Yes	120-480degress F Up to One Hour
Roast	400 Degrees F 1 Hour Convection	Yes	>390 Degrees F For 4 Hours 300-390degrees F For 8 Hours 210-300 Degrees F For 12 Hours
Preheat	325 Degrees F 18 Minutes Super Convection Frozen Food	No	120-480 Degrees F Up to 1 hour
Proof	85 Degrees F 1 Hour Convection	Yes	80-100 Degrees F Up To 2 Hours
Air Fry	400 Degrees F 18 Minutes Super Convection Frozen Foods	Yes	120 -480 Degrees F (Up to One Hour)
Dehydrate	125degreesf 12 Hours Super Convection	No	86-176 Degrees F (Up to 72 Hours)
Cookies	325 Degrees F 11 Minutes Convection	Yes	120 -480 Degrees F (Up to One Hour)
Reheat	325 Degrees F 15 Minutes Convection	No	120 -480 Degrees F (Up to Two Hour)
Slow Cook	HIGH 4 Hours Convection	Yes	High:2-12Hr Low:4-72 Hr Auto: Keep Warm 2 Hours

Benefits of Using Breville Smart Air Fryer Toast Oven

- It is a versatile product where we can cook different things, because it is also a combination of air fryer, oven and dehydrator.
- It is a very powerful oven and can prepare a huge variety of food quickly.
- Its two-speed fan provides a large amount of air to ensure even heat distribution during frying, dehydration and roasting.
- It is equipped with PID temperature control technology and able to move. the temperature to where it is most needed.
- Its construction material is stainless steel which is perfect for preventing from messy cooking.
- It provides odor-free cooking.
- It is a timesaving appliance.

Tips and Cautions of Breville Smart Air Fryer Toast Oven Usage

Whenever an electric appliance is used, there should be some tips and caution that needed to be followed:

- First step is to remove the packaging and promotional labels.
- Remove safety fitting on the power plug to avoid a hazard.
- Ensure the space or surface where the oven is place is stable, leveled, and heat resistance.
- Don't put appliance near curtains or cloth-covered surface.
- Don't store or put any decoration or item over the top of the oven.
- Don't use the appliance on a burner or hot gas.
- Do not immerse cords or plug in water.
- The appliance should be at a distance of 15cm from the walls.
- Oversized utensils or trays should not be inserted in the oven.
- Do not cover the trays with metal foil, when putting inside the oven.
- Don't let the door of the oven open for a longer period.
- The appliance is for household use, so it should not be used inside the vehicle or outdoor.
- Before cleaning the appliance unplug all the cables and plugs.
- Don't use a metal scouring pad for cleaning the oven.
- Check the accessories if maintained or replacement needed.

Cooking Timetable

Cooking Items	Temperature Range	Cooking Time
Green Vegetables	400 Degrees	5- Minutes
Onion ring	390 Degrees F	6 Minutes
Potato	400 Degrees F	15-40 Minutes
Zucchini	400 Degrees F	12 Minutes
Eggplant	400 Degrees F	15 Minutes
Chicken Breast	370 Degrees F	20 -25 Minutes
Chicken Thigh	380 Degrees F	22 -25 Minutes
Drumstick	370-400 Degrees F	20-25 Minutes
Flank Steak (Beef)	400 Degrees F	12 Minutes
Meatballs	380 Degrees F	7 -10 Minutes
Fish	400 Degrees F	10 Minutes
Salmon	380-400 Degrees F	10-12 Minutes
Bacon	400 Degrees F	5 -7 Minutes
Pork	360-400 Degrees F	12 Minutes
French Fries	400 Degrees F	15 Minutes
Lamb	400 Degrees F	12 Minutes

Chapter 2: Breakfast Recipes

Breakfast Bombs

Explode with satisfaction with these breakfast bombs.
Prep Time and Cooking Time: 20 minutes | Serves: 6

Ingredients to Use:

- 1 cup scrambled eggs
- 1/2 cup cheddar cheese, shredded
- 1/2 cup bacon, cooked and crumbled
- 1 package refrigerator biscuits
- Salt and pepper to taste
- Cooking spray

Step-by-Step Directions

1. In a bowl, combine the eggs, cheese and bacon.
2. Place in the center of the biscuits.
3. Season with salt and pepper.
4. Roll and seal the edges.
5. Add to the air fryer oven.
6. Spray with oil.
7. Choose toast setting.
8. Toast at 330 degrees F for 5 minutes.

Serving Suggestion:

Serve with hot chocolate drink.

Tip:

You can also use mozzarella cheese for this recipe.

Vegetable Frittata

This vegetable frittata is loaded with flavors and textures that you love.
Prep Time and Cooking Time: 15 minutes | Serves: 6

Ingredients to Use:

- 4 eggs, beaten
- 1/4 cup leek, chopped
- 1 cup spinach, chopped
- 1 cup mushrooms, sliced
- 3 tablespoons heavy cream
- 1/2 cup cheddar cheese, shredded
- 1 teaspoon garlic salt
- Salt and pepper to taste

Step-by-Step Directions

1. Mix all the ingredients in a bowl.
2. Pour mixture into a small baking pan.
3. Slide the baking pan into the air fryer oven.
4. Opt for air fry setting.
5. Air fry at 300 degrees F for 10 minutes.

Serving Suggestion:

Garnish with chopped chives.

Tip:

You can also add other vegetables into the mix.

Sausage Patties

If you want something heavy for breakfast, try these delicious sausage patties.
Prep Time and Cooking Time: 15 minutes | Serves: 8

Ingredients to Use:

- 1 package thawed sausage patties

Step-by-Step Directions

1. Spread the sausage patties on the air fryer tray.
2. Set it to air fry.
3. Cook at 400 degrees F for 5 minutes.

4. Flip and cook for another 5 minutes.

Serving Suggestion:

Garnish with parsley.

Tip:

Thaw the sausages before air frying.

Breakfast Burrito

Enjoy Mexican flavors with this delicious breakfast burrito.

Prep Time and Cooking Time: 30 minutes | Serves: 4

Ingredients to Use:

- 4 scrambled eggs
- 1 lb. ground sausage, cooked and crumbled
- 1/2 cup red bell pepper, chopped
- 4 tortillas
- 1/2 cup salsa
- 1/2 cup cheese, shredded

Step-by-Step Directions

1. Mix the eggs, sausage and red bell pepper.
2. Add this mixture on top of the tortillas.
3. Sprinkle with cheese.
4. Roll up the tortillas.
5. Select air fry option.
6. Cook at 400 degrees F for 5 minutes.
7. Spread the salsa on top.

Serving Suggestion:

Garnish with basil leaves.

Tip:

Use Colby Jack cheese for this recipe.

Chocolate French Toast

A rich and delicious breakfast toast that only takes a few minutes to prepare.

Prep Time and Cooking Time: 20 minutes | Serves: 4

Ingredients to Use:

- 4 eggs, beaten
- 1 cup milk
- 1/4 cup cocoa powder
- 1/2 cup sugar
- 1/2 teaspoon baking powder
- Pinch salt
- 8 slices bread, cut into strips

Step-by-Step Directions

1. Mix the eggs, milk, cocoa powder, sugar, baking powder and salt in a bowl.
2. Dip the bread slices in the mixture.
3. Let it soak for 5 minutes.
4. Transfer to the air fryer oven.
5. Choose toast setting.
6. Cook at 350 degrees F for 5 minutes per side.

Serving Suggestion:

Dust with powdered sugar.

Tip:

Use unsweetened cocoa powder.

Sausage Muffin

Craving for your favorite fast food breakfast? Here's how to make your own at home.

Prep Time and Cooking Time: 15 minutes | Serves: 2

Ingredients to Use:

- 2 sausage patties
- 2 English muffins, split in half
- 2 tablespoons butter, softened
- 2 slices cheddar cheese

Step-by-Step Directions

1. Place the sausage patties in the air fryer oven.
2. Set it to toast.
3. Cook at 400 degrees F for 5 minutes per side.
4. Brush the muffins with the softened

butter.

5. In the last 3 minutes of cooking the sausages, add the muffins.
6. Place the muffins on a plate.
7. Top with the cheese and sausages.
8. Top with the other muffin slice.

Serving Suggestion:

Serve with a cup of hot coffee.

Sweet Potato Hash

There's so much to love about this dish—its flavors and aroma are truly enticing.

Prep Time and Cooking Time: 25 minutes | Serves: 4

Ingredients to Use:

- 2 cups sweet potatoes, diced
- 3 slices bacon, chopped
- 3 tablespoons olive oil
- 1 teaspoon sweet paprika
- 1 teaspoon Italian seasoning
- Salt and pepper to taste

Step-by-Step Directions

1. Combine all the ingredients in a bowl.
2. Mix well.
3. Transfer to the air fryer oven.
4. Select roast setting.
5. Roast at 400 degrees F for 15 minutes, stirring twice.

Serving Suggestion:

Sprinkle with pepper.

Tip:

Spread the sweet potatoes in a single layer to cook evenly.

Egg in Hole Sandwich

Impress your family with this interesting yet easy to make breakfast dish.

Prep Time and Cooking Time: 15 minutes | Serves: 4

Ingredients to Use:

- 4 teaspoons butter, softened
- 4 slices bread
- 4 eggs
- Salt and pepper to taste

Step-by-Step Directions

1. Spread the butter on top of the breads slices.
2. Cut a hole in the center using a cookie or biscuit cutter.
3. Place the bread slices on the air crisper.
4. Crack the eggs into the holes of the bread.
5. Set your air fryer oven to toast.
6. Toast at 330 degrees F for 5 to 7 minutes.

Serving Suggestion:

Sprinkle with chopped green onion.

Tip:

Any type of bread can be used for this recipe.

Sausages

A classic breakfast dish that's perfect for busy mornings.

Prep Time and Cooking Time: 15 minutes | Serves: 10

Ingredients to Use:

- 1 package breakfast sausage

Step-by-Step Directions

1. Arrange the sausages on the air fryer tray.
2. Select air fry setting.
3. Cook at 400 degrees F for 5 minutes.
4. Flip and cook for another 5 minutes.

Serving Suggestion:

Serve with hash browns.

Tip:

Poke the sausages with a fork before air frying.

Hash Browns

Here's a quick and easy breakfast dish that would certainly fill you up.
Prep Time and Cooking Time: 15 minutes | Serves: 6

Ingredients to Use:

- Cooking spray
- 6 frozen hash browns

Step-by-Step Directions

1. Spray your air crisper tray with oil.
2. Arrange the hash browns in the air crisper tray.
3. Turn to air fry setting.
4. Cook at 400 degrees F for 5 minutes.
5. Flip and cook for another 5 minutes.

Serving Suggestion:

Serve with ketchup and mayo.

Tip:

Do not overcrowd your air crisper tray.

Banana Bread

This banana bread comes out nice and fluffy when you cook it in your air fryer oven.
Prep Time and Cooking Time: 40 minutes | Serves: 4

Ingredients to Use:

- 2 cups flour
- 1 egg, beaten
- 1-1/4 cup sugar
- 1 teaspoon baking soda
- Pinch salt
- 2 tablespoons milk
- 1 teaspoon vanilla extract
- 1/2 cup vegetable oil
- 3 ripe bananas, mashed

Step-by-Step Directions

1. Combine flour, egg, sugar, baking soda and salt in a bowl.
2. Mix well.
3. Stir in the milk, vanilla extract and oil.
4. Mix until fully combined.
5. Add the mashed bananas and mix well.
6. Pour the batter into a small loaf pan.
7. Place the pan inside the air fryer oven.
8. Choose bake function.
9. Bake at 310 degrees F for 30 minutes.

Serving Suggestion:

Let cool for 5 to 10 minutes before slicing and serving.

Tip:

Check for doneness by inserting a toothpick into the bread. If it comes out clean, then it means that the bread is already cooked.

Strawberry Oatmeal

Make your oatmeal more flavorful by topping it with strawberries.
Prep Time and Cooking Time: 40 minutes | Serves: 2

Ingredients to Use:

- 2 cups strawberries, sliced and divided
- 1 cup milk
- 1 cup rolled oats
- 4 tablespoons brown sugar
- 1/2 teaspoon ground cinnamon
- 1/2 teaspoon baking powder
- 4 tablespoons almonds, slivered
- Pinch salt

Step-by-Step Directions

1. Combine half of the strawberries with the rest of the ingredients in a small baking pan.
2. Let sit for 10 minutes.
3. Sprinkle the remaining strawberries on top.
4. Place the pan inside the air fryer oven.
5. Turn to bake function.
6. Bake at 350 degrees F for 10 minutes,

stirring once.

Serving Suggestion:

Sprinkle with nutmeg before serving.

Tip:

You can also add 1 egg into the mixture.

Buttered Bagel

Who can say no to buttered bagel in the morning?
Prep Time and Cooking Time: 10 minutes | Serves: 2

Ingredients to Use:

- 2 tablespoons butter, softened
- 2 bagels, sliced in half

Step-by-Step Directions

1. Spread half of the butter on the bagels.
2. Place inside the air fryer oven.
3. Set your air fryer oven to toast.
4. Toast at 365 degrees F for 3 minutes.
5. Take the bagels out of the oven.
6. Spread remaining butter.
7. Toast for another 3 minutes.

Serving Suggestion:

Serve with coffee or hot chocolate drink.

Grilled Cheese Sandwich

This grilled cheese sandwich is always a good idea for breakfast!
Prep Time and Cooking Time: 10 minutes | Serves: 2

Ingredients to Use:

- 2 tablespoons butter, softened
- 4 slices bread
- 8 slices provolone cheese
- 2 eggs, fried

Step-by-Step Directions

1. Spread butter on the bread slices.
2. Add the cheese slices on top of the 2 bread slices.
3. Preheat your air fryer oven to 350 degrees F for 5 minutes.
4. Choose toast setting.
5. Toast all the bread slices inside the oven for 3 minutes.
6. Take the bread slices out of the oven.
7. Add the egg on top.
8. Top with the other bread slice.

Serving Suggestion:

Serve with hot drink.

Tip:

You can skip the egg to reduce calorie count if you like.

Chocolate Croissant

These chocolate drizzled croissants are perfect whether for breakfast or for snack.
Prep Time and Cooking Time: 15 minutes | Serves: 8

Ingredients to Use:

- 1 pack frozen croissant rolls
- 4 tablespoons chocolate syrup

Step-by-Step Directions

1. Add the croissant rolls to the air fryer oven.
2. Choose air fry setting.
3. Cook at 320 degrees F for 4 to 5 minutes per side or until golden.
4. Drizzle with the chocolate syrup and serve.

Serving Suggestion:

Sprinkle with chopped walnuts on top.

Tip:

You can also use canned croissant rolls.

Blueberry Buckle

Want something sweet but healthy for breakfast? Here's the perfect choice.

Prep Time and Cooking Time: 30 minutes | Serves: 6

Ingredients to Use:

- Cooking spray
- Cake
- 2 cups cake mix
- 3/4 cup butter, melted
- 14 oz. condensed milk
- 1-3/4 cup blueberries
- 1 teaspoon lemon zest
- Topping
- 1/2 cup cake mix
- 2 tablespoons butter, melted
- 1/2 cup brown sugar

Step-by-Step Directions

1. Combine the cake ingredients in a bowl.
2. Mix well.
3. Spray a small cake pan with oil.
4. Pour the batter into the cake pan.
5. Blend the topping ingredients in another bowl.
6. Spread this mixture on top of the batter.
7. Place the pan inside the air fryer oven.
8. Turn to bake option.
9. Cook at 320 degrees F for 10 minutes.

Serving Suggestion:

Drizzle with syrup before serving.

Tip:

Check for doneness by inserting a toothpick into the bread. If it comes out clean, then it means that the bread is already cooked.

Cinnamon Roll French Toast

This can easily become a family favorite. It's very easy to make too.

Prep Time and Cooking Time: 15 minutes | Serves: 6

Ingredients to Use:

- Cooking spray
- 6 cinnamon rolls
- 3 eggs
- 1 teaspoon vanilla extract
- 1 cup milk

Step-by-Step Directions

1. Spray your baking pan with oil.
2. Add the cinnamon rolls to the air fryer oven.
3. Choose toast setting.
4. Toast at 350 degrees F for 7 minutes.
5. Take out of the oven.
6. Let cool for 10 minutes.
7. In a bowl, beat the eggs.
8. Stir in the vanilla extract and milk.
9. Soak the cinnamon rolls in the mixture.
10. Place these back to the air fryer.
11. Toast at 340 degrees F for 3 minutes per side.

Serving Suggestion:

Dust with confectioners' sugar.

Tip:

You can also make your own cinnamon rolls if you prefer but to save time, it would be a good idea to buy these pre-made.

Breakfast Pinwheels

You'll be delighted to learn how to make these awesome pinwheels for breakfast.

Prep Time and Cooking Time: 20 minutes | Serves: 6

Ingredients to Use:

- 1 pack crescent rounds
- 1/2 cup cheddar cheese, grated
- 3 slices bacon, cooked

Step-by-Step Directions

1. Unroll the crescent rounds.
2. Sprinkle the grated cheddar cheese on top.
3. Top with the bacon.
4. Roll up the crescent rounds.

5. Add to the air fryer oven.
6. Choose air fry setting.
7. Cook at 330 degrees F for 5 minutes.
8. Flip and cook for another 2 minutes.

Serving Suggestion:

Sprinkle with a little pepper.

Tip:

You can also brush the tops with melted butter before air frying.

Loaded Omelette

This bright and colorful omelette will surely brighten up the rest of your day.
Prep Time and Cooking Time: 20 minutes | Serves: 2

Ingredients to Use:

- 2 eggs
- 1/4 cup milk
- Pinch salt
- 1 onion, chopped
- 1 red bell pepper, diced
- 1 green bell pepper, diced
- 1/4 cup cheddar cheese, shredded
- 1 ham, diced
- 1 teaspoon Italian seasoning

Step-by-Step Directions

1. Beat the eggs and milk in a bowl.
2. Season with salt.
3. Stir in the rest of the ingredients.
4. Pour into a small baking pan.
5. Place inside the air fryer oven.
6. Set it to air fry.
7. Cook at 350 degrees F for 10 minutes.

Serving Suggestion:

Sprinkle chopped scallions on top.

Tip:

You can also add mushrooms to the mixture.

Scrambled Eggs with Mushrooms

Make your scrambled eggs without any fuss using your air fryer.
Prep Time and Cooking Time: 15 minutes | Serves: 2

Ingredients to Use:

- 2 eggs, beaten
- 2 tablespoons milk
- 1/4 tablespoon butter, melted
- 1/8 cup cheddar cheese, shredded
- 1/4 cup mushrooms
- Salt and pepper to taste

Step-by-Step Directions

1. Add the eggs to a bowl.
2. Stir in the rest of the ingredients.
3. Add the mixture to a baking pan.
4. Place baking pan inside the air fryer oven.
5. Choose air fry setting.
6. Set temperature to 300 degrees F.
7. Cook for 3 minutes.
8. Stir and cook for another 3 minutes.
9. Stir again and cook until eggs are set.

Serving Suggestion:

Sprinkle with chopped green onions.

Tip:

Use sliced button mushrooms for this recipe.

Chapter 3: Beef Dishes

Sirloin Steak with Mustard Butter

This is one quick and simple dish that you can't get enough.

Prep Time and Cooking Time: 20 minutes | Serves: 2

Ingredients to Use:

- 2 sirloin steaks
- 2 tablespoons olive oil
- Salt and pepper to taste
- Mustard butter
- 2 tablespoons butter
- 1 tablespoon scallion, chopped
- 1 teaspoon mustard
- Salt and pepper to taste

Step-by-Step Directions

1. Preheat your air fryer to 400 degrees F for 5 minutes.
2. Brush steaks with oil.
3. Season with salt and pepper.
4. Choose air fry setting in your air fryer oven.
5. Cook the steaks for 6 minutes per side.
6. Mix the mustard butter ingredients in a bowl.
7. Press onto a small circular dish.
8. Cover and refrigerate for 1 hour.
9. Top the steaks with the mustard butter and serve.

Serving Suggestion:

Serve with steamed or grilled asparagus.

Tip:

Use Dijon style mustard.

Bourbon Steaks

Add bourbon to your steaks and you'll be surprised with the outcome.

Prep Time and Cooking Time: 1 hour and 20 minutes | Serves: 4

Ingredients to Use:

- 1 lb. steak, sliced into cubes

Marinade

- 1/2 cup vegetable oil
- 1/2 cup bourbon
- 1/2 cup Worcestershire sauce
- 1/2 cup mustard
- 1/2 cup brown sugar

Step-by-Step Directions

1. Mix the marinade ingredients in a bowl.
2. Add the steak cubes to the marinade.
3. Cover and marinate for 1 hour in the refrigerator.
4. Transfer steak cubes to the air fryer tray.
5. Select grill setting.
6. Set it to 400 degrees F.
7. Cook for 5 minutes.
8. Turn and cook for another 5 minutes.

Serving Suggestion:

Serve with vegetable side dish.

Tip:

You can also use honey instead of brown sugar.

Rib Eye Steak with Buttered Garlic & Chives

Make your herbed butter with garlic and chives for incredible flavors you'd love.

Prep Time and Cooking Time: 1 hour and 20

minutes | Serves: 2

Ingredients to Use:

- 2 rib eye steaks
- Olive oil
- Salt and pepper to taste
- Garlic & chive butter
- 1/2 cup butter
- 1 clove garlic, minced
- 1 tablespoon chives, chopped

Step-by-Step Directions

1. Combine the butter ingredients in a bowl.
2. Refrigerate for 1 hour.
3. Preheat your air fryer to 400 degrees F for 5 minutes.
4. Rub steaks with oil and season with salt and pepper.
5. Place inside the air fryer oven.
6. Choose air fry option.
7. Air fry the steaks for 6 minutes.
8. Turn and cook for another 6 minutes.
9. Top the steaks with the butter compound and serve.

Serving Suggestion:

Serve with gravy.

Tip:

You can also use other types of steaks for this recipe.

Sesame Beef Stir Fry

There's no need for Chinese takeout when you can make this fantastic dish at home.
Prep Time and Cooking Time: 15 minutes | Serves: 2

Ingredients to Use:

Stir Fry

- 1 lb. flank steak, sliced into strips
- 1/2 cup red onions, sliced
- 1/2 cup carrots, shredded
- 1/2 cup snow peas
- 1/2 cup broccoli florets

Sauce

- 2 cloves garlic, minced
- 1/4 cup hoisin sauce
- 1 tablespoon soy sauce
- 1 teaspoon ground ginger
- 1 teaspoon sesame oil
- 1/4 cup water

Step-by-Step Directions

1. Preheat your air fryer to 400 degrees F for 5 minutes.
2. Choose grill setting.
3. Mix the sauce ingredients in a bowl. Set aside.
4. Add the steaks to the air fryer tray.
5. Cook for 5 minutes per side.
6. Stir in the rest of the stir fry ingredients.
7. Cook for 3 minutes.
8. Add the sauce and stir.
9. Cook for 7 minutes, stirring once or twice.

Serving Suggestion:

Garnish with sesame seeds.

Tip:

Stir to make sure that the steak and veggies do not stick to the air fryer basket.

Steak with Pastrami Butter

Making steak has never been this easy!
Prep Time and Cooking Time: 20 minutes | Serves: 2

Ingredients to Use:

- 2 sirloin steaks
- 2 tablespoons butter
- Salt and pepper to taste
- 1/4 cup butter
- 2 teaspoons pastrami spice blend

Step-by-Step Directions

- Preheat your air fryer oven to 400 degrees F for 5 minutes.
- Spread 2 tablespoons butter on both sides of steaks.
- Sprinkle with salt and pepper.
- Place the steaks inside the air fryer oven.
- Turn to air fry setting.
- Cook steaks for 6 minutes per side.
- Mix the butter and pastrami spice blend.
- Serve on top of the steaks.

Serving Suggestion:

Serve with green leafy salad.

Tip:

Let steak rest for 10 minutes at room temperature before seasoning.

Garlic Steak with Creamy Horseradish

This is a no-fuss steak dish that you can cook quickly in the air fryer.
Prep Time and Cooking Time: 30 minutes | Serves: 2

Ingredients to Use:

- 2 sirloin steaks
- 2 tablespoons olive oil
- 2 cloves garlic, minced
- Salt and pepper to taste

Creamy horseradish

- 2 tablespoons horseradish
- 1 cup sour cream
- 1 teaspoon dill
- Salt and pepper to taste

Step-by-Step Directions

1. Brush both sides of steak with oil.
2. Sprinkle with garlic, salt and pepper.
3. Select roast setting.
4. Place the steaks inside the air fryer oven.
5. Cook the steaks for 6 minutes per side.
6. In a bowl, mix the creamy horseradish ingredients.
7. Spread on top of steaks and serve.

Serving Suggestion:

Serve on top of sautéed spinach.

Tip:

You can also use prime rib for this recipe.

Beef Taco

Enjoy Mexican flavors with this easy to make beef taco recipe.
Prep Time and Cooking Time: 20 minutes | Serves: 4

Ingredients to Use:

- 1 lb. ground beef
- 1 tablespoon taco seasoning
- 4 corn tortillas
- Cilantro slaw
- 1 red onion, chopped
- 1 clove garlic, minced
- 2 tablespoons fresh cilantro, chopped
- 1 cup cabbage, shredded
- 1 tablespoon olive oil
- 2 teaspoons lime juice

Step-by-Step Directions

1. Add the ground beef to a small baking pan.
2. Sprinkle with taco seasoning and mix.
3. Place inside the air fryer oven.
4. Choose air fry setting.
5. Air fry at 400 degrees F for 5 minutes.
6. Stir and cook for another 5 minutes.
7. Toss the cilantro slaw in a bowl.
8. Top the tortilla with the beef mixture and cilantro slaw.
9. Fold and serve.

Serving Suggestion:

Serve with sour cream.

Tip:

You can also use flour tortilla for this recipe.

Strip Steak with Boursin Cheese

Your house will seem like a fancy restaurant once you make this awesome steak dish.
Prep Time and Cooking Time: 20 minutes | Serves: 2

Ingredients to Use:

- 2 strip steaks
- Olive oil
- Salt and pepper to taste
- Boursin Cheese
- 12 oz. cream cheese
- 1 clove garlic, minced
- 1 teaspoon parsley, chopped
- 1 teaspoon dried marjoram
- 1 teaspoon dried basil
- 1 teaspoon dried oregano
- 1 teaspoon dried sage
- 1 teaspoon dried chives

Step-by-Step Directions

1. Coat steaks with oil.
2. Season with salt and pepper.
3. Add to the air fryer oven.
4. Set it to grill or roast.
5. Cook at 400 degrees F for 6 minutes per side.
6. Mix boursin cheese ingredients in a bowl.
7. Serve steak with the boursin cheese on top.

Serving Suggestion:

Serve with roasted baby potatoes.

Tip:

Use New York strip steaks if available.

Baked Meatballs

You and your family will surely be delighted with this amazing dish.
Prep Time and Cooking Time: 15 minutes | Serves: 4

Ingredients to Use:

- 16 oz. frozen meatballs
- 14 oz. marinara sauce
- 1/2 cup mozzarella cheese

Step-by-Step Directions

1. Spread marinara sauce on top of a baking pan.
2. Add meatballs on top.
3. Place the pan inside the air fryer oven.
4. Choose bake function.
5. Set it to 340 degrees F.
6. Cook for 10 minutes.
7. Sprinkle mozzarella cheese over the meatballs.
8. Cook for another 5 minutes.

Serving Suggestion:

Garnish with fresh basil leaves.

Tip:

Use low-sodium marinara sauce.

Pepper Kebabs

Here's a delicious twist to your favorite beef kebab.
Prep Time and Cooking Time: 2 hour and 30 minutes | Serves: 4

Ingredients to Use:

- 1 lb. sirloin steak, sliced into cubes
- 1 bell pepper, sliced
- 1 onion, sliced

Marinade

- 1 clove garlic, minced
- 1/4 cup soy sauce
- 2 tablespoons olive oil
- 2 tablespoons vinegar
- 1 teaspoon ginger, grated
- Pepper to taste

Step-by-Step Directions

1. Mix the marinade ingredients in a bowl.
2. Transfer half of the mixture to another bowl.
3. Marinate steak slices in the first bowl and the veggies in the second bowl for 2 hours.
4. Thread beef and veggies onto skewers.
5. Place inside the air fryer oven.
6. Choose air fry setting.
7. Cook at 350 degrees F for 5 minutes per side.

Serving Suggestion:

Serve with grilled vegetables.

Tip:

Use red wine vinegar if available.

Garlic Parmesan Strip Steak

Make your compound butter with garlic and Parmesan for unforgettable steak.
Prep Time and Cooking Time: 20 minutes | Serves: 2

Ingredients to Use:

- Steaks
- 2 strip steaks
- 1 teaspoon olive oil
- Salt and pepper to taste
- Garlic Parmesan butter
- 2 teaspoons garlic, minced
- 1/2 cup butter
- 1/4 cup Parmesan cheese, grated

Step-by-Step Directions

1. Brush both sides of steaks with olive oil.
2. Place inside the air fryer oven.
3. Select air fry option.
4. Air fry for 5 minutes per side.
5. Mix garlic, butter and cheese in a bowl.
6. Form butter mixture into a round shape.
7. Refrigerate until firm.
8. Top steaks with the butter.

Serving Suggestion:

Let rest for 5 minutes before serving.

Tip:

Use New York strip steaks.

Pepper Steak with Veggies

This is as delicious as it is colorful!
Prep Time and Cooking Time: 1 hour and 15 minutes | Serves: 4

Ingredients to Use:

- 1 tablespoon olive oil
- 1/4 cup soy sauce
- 1 lb. flank steak, sliced into strips
- 2 cloves garlic, minced
- 1 teaspoon ground ginger
- Salt and pepper to taste
- 1 red bell pepper, sliced into strips
- 1 green bell pepper, sliced into strips
- 1 yellow bell pepper, sliced into strips

Step-by-Step Directions

1. Combine all ingredients except bell peppers in a sealable plastic bag.
2. Seal and refrigerate for 1 hour.
3. Add beef to the air crisper tray.
4. Select roast setting.
5. Cook at 400 degrees F for 10 minutes.
6. Stir and add the bell peppers.
7. Cook for another 5 minutes.

Serving Suggestion:

Serve on top of white rice.

Tip:

Slice steak against the grain.

Pepper & Thyme Steak

Flavor up your flank steak with thyme and pepper.

Prep Time and Cooking Time: 10 minutes | Serves: 4

Ingredients to Use:

- 2 tablespoons olive oil
- 1 teaspoon thyme, chopped
- 1 tablespoon lemon zest
- 4 tablespoons soy sauce
- Salt and pepper to taste
- 1 lb. flank steak

Step-by-Step Directions

1. Combine all the ingredients except flank steak in a bowl.
2. Brush both sides of steaks with this mixture.
3. Place steaks inside the air fryer oven.
4. Select roast function.
5. Cook at 400 degrees F for 7 to 10 minutes per side.

Serving Suggestion:

Serve with salad.

Tip:

Add 2 more minutes cooking time for well done.

Greek Burger

Take a trip to Greece when you make this burger at your home.
Prep Time and Cooking Time: 20 minutes | Serves: 4

Ingredients to Use:

- 1-1/2 lb. ground beef
- 1 clove garlic, minced
- 1 tablespoon fresh oregano, chopped
- 1/2 cup feta cheese
- 1 tablespoon lemon juice

Step-by-Step Directions

1. Combine all ingredients in a bowl.
2. Form patties from the mixture.
3. Add these to the air fryer oven.
4. Choose air fry setting.
5. Cook at 380 degrees F for 5 minutes per side.

Serving Suggestion:

Serve in burger buns with lettuce and tomatoes.

Tip:

You can swap garlic with garlic powder.

Bacon Wrapped Beef Tenderloin

You don't have to be a kitchen pro to make this amazing dish.
Prep Time and Cooking Time: 20 minutes | Serves: 2

Ingredients to Use:

- 2 beef tenderloin fillets
- Salt and pepper to taste
- 2 slices bacon

Step-by-Step Directions

1. Season beef with salt and pepper.
2. Wrap bacon around the beef.
3. Set your air fryer oven to air fry.
4. Cook at 400 degrees F for 6 minutes per side.

Serving Suggestion:

Drizzle with steak sauce before serving.

Tip:

Use a toothpick to secure the bacon.

Blue Cheese Burger

This is a surprisingly easy burger dish that you'd enjoy making.
Prep Time and Cooking Time: 20 minutes | Serves: 15

Ingredients to Use:

- 3 lb. lean ground beef
- 1/8 cup chives, minced

- 4 oz. blue cheese
- 1 teaspoon Worcestershire sauce
- 1/4 teaspoon hot pepper sauce
- Salt and pepper to taste

Step-by-Step Directions

1. Combine all the ingredients in a bowl.
2. Form patties from the mixture.
3. Add patties to the air fryer oven.
4. Cook the patties at 360 degrees F for 6 minutes.
5. Flip and cook for another 5 to 7 minutes.

Serving Suggestion:

Serve in burger buns with lettuce and tomatoes.

Tip:

Make sure burger patty is fully cooked. Extend cooking time if necessary.

Carne Asada

This isn't like any other dish you've ever taste.
Prep Time and Cooking Time: 30 minutes | Serves: 6

Ingredients to Use:

- 1/4 cup olive oil
- 1/4 cup lime juice
- 1/2 cup cilantro, chopped
- 4 cloves garlic, minced
- 1 teaspoon cumin powder
- 1 teaspoon chili powder
- Salt and pepper to taste
- 1-1/2 lb. flank steak

Step-by-Step Directions

1. Combine all the ingredients except flank steak in a bowl.
2. Mix well.
3. Add the flank steak to the bowl.
4. Coat evenly with the marinade.
5. Cover and marinate for 1 hour in the refrigerator.
6. Transfer the steak to the air fryer oven.
7. Choose roast setting.
8. Cook at 400 degrees F for 7 minutes per side.

Serving Suggestion:

Serve with salad.

Tip:

Internal temperature should be 145 degrees F.

Hoisin Meatballs

These meatballs are bursting with so much flavor.
Prep Time and Cooking Time: 20 minutes | Serves: 6

Ingredients to Use:

- 1 lb. lean ground beef
- 2 tablespoons scallions, chopped
- 2 tablespoons ginger, minced
- 1 teaspoon sugar
- 2 teaspoons garlic powder
- 1 egg, beaten
- 1/2 cup breadcrumbs
- 1/2 cup hoisin sauce
- Cooking spray

Step-by-Step Directions

1. Mix all the ingredients except hoisin sauce in a bowl.
2. Form meatballs from the mixture.
3. Spray with oil.
4. Transfer to the air fryer oven.
5. Select roast setting.
6. Cook at 350 degrees F for 6 minutes per side.
7. Toss in hoisin sauce and serve.

Serving Suggestion:

Garnish with toasted sesame seeds.

Tip:

Use lean ground beef.

Fried Steak

Want crispy steak? Here's how to do it right.
Prep Time and Cooking Time: 30 minutes | Serves: 4

Ingredients to Use:

- 4 steaks
- Salt and pepper to taste
- 1 cup flour
- 1 egg, beaten
- 1/4 cup milk
- 1 cup breadcrumbs
- Cooking spray

Step-by-Step Directions

1. Season steaks with salt and pepper.
2. Cover with flour.
3. Dip in egg mixed with milk.
4. Dredge with breadcrumbs.
5. Spray with oil.
6. Place steaks in the air fryer tray.
7. Choose air fry setting.
8. Cook at 400 degrees F for 5 minutes per side.

Serving Suggestion:

Serve with mashed potatoes and gravy.

Tip:

Use prime rib or rib eye steaks.

Steak Fajitas

This dish is overflowing with color and flavor.
Prep Time and Cooking Time: 3 hours and 30 minutes | Serves: 4

Ingredients to Use:

- 1 lb. flank steak, sliced into strips

Marinade

- 4 cloves garlic, minced
- 2 tablespoons olive oil
- 1/4 cup lime juice
- 2 teaspoons soy sauce
- 1/4 cup water
- 1/2 teaspoon cayenne pepper
- 1/2 teaspoon liquid smoke flavoring
- Salt and pepper to taste

Vegetables

- 1 red bell pepper, sliced into strips
- 1 orange bell pepper, sliced into strips
- 1 yellow bell pepper, sliced into strips
- 1 sweet onion, sliced into strips

Step-by-Step Directions

1. Combine marinade ingredients in a bowl.
2. Stir in the beef strips.
3. Cover and marinate for 3 hours.
4. Add steak and vegetables to the air fryer oven.
5. Select bake setting.
6. Cook at 400 degrees F for 10 minutes.
7. Stir and cook for another 10 minutes.

Serving Suggestion:

Serve on top of tortillas.

Tip:

Slice beef against the grain.

Steak Tips

Tender fall-off-the-bone steak tips—something you'd love to have for dinner.
Prep Time and Cooking Time: 2 hours and 15 minutes | Serves: 4

Ingredients to Use:

- 2 lb. rib eye steak, sliced into cubes
- Marinade
- 1 tablespoon olive oil
- 1 teaspoon onion powder
- 1 teaspoon garlic powder
- 2 teaspoons steak seasoning

- Salt and pepper to taste

Step-by-Step Directions

1. Combine marinade ingredients in a bowl.
2. Marinate beef for 2 hours.
3. Transfer beef to the air fryer tray.
4. Turn to air fry setting.
5. Cook at 400 degrees F for 4 minutes.
6. Turn the beef and cook for another 3 minutes.

Serving Suggestion:

Serve with mashed potatoes and gravy.

Tip:

You can also use butter instead of olive oil.

Korean Short Ribs

Take your taste buds to a trip to Korea with this amazing recipe.
Prep Time and Cooking Time: 1 hour and 10 minutes | Serves: 4

Ingredients to Use:

- 2 lb. beef short ribs
- 1 teaspoon garlic, minced
- 1/2 teaspoon red pepper flakes
- 1 tablespoon ground ginger
- 1/2 cup brown sugar
- 1/2 cup soy sauce

Step-by-Step Directions

1. Combine all the ingredients in a bowl.
2. Cover and marinate for 1 hour.
3. Add to the air fryer oven.
4. Select air fry option.
5. Cook at 400 degrees F for 5 minutes.
6. Brush with marinade and flip.
7. Cook for another 5 minutes.

Serving Suggestion:

Garnish with chopped scallions.

Tip:

You can also use honey instead of sugar.

Beef & Spinach Rolls

It takes quite some effort to make these beef and spinach rolls, but they are surely worth it.
Prep Time and Cooking Time: 20 minutes | Serves: 2

Ingredients to Use:

- 2 beef tenderloin fillets
- Salt and pepper to taste
- 1 cup spinach, sliced
- 1/2 cup garlic herb cream chees

Step-by-Step Directions

1. Season beef with salt and pepper.
2. In a bowl, mix spinach and garlic herb cream cheese.
3. Spread mixture on top of the beef.
4. Roll up the beef.
5. Place in the air fryer tray.
6. Choose air fry setting.
7. Set it to 400 degrees F.
8. Cook for 6 minutes per side.

Serving Suggestion:

Serve with green salad.

Tip:

Flatten beef with meat mallet.

Chapter 4: Pork Dishes

Pork Chops with Broccoli

This complete meal is ready in only 15 minutes.
Prep Time and Cooking Time: 15 minutes | Serves: 2

Ingredients to Use:

- 2 pork chops
- 2 tablespoons avocado oil, divided
- 1/2 teaspoon onion powder
- 1/2 teaspoon garlic powder
- 1/2 teaspoon paprika
- 2 cups broccoli florets
- 2 cloves garlic, minced
- Salt to taste

Step-by-Step Directions

1. Preheat your air fryer to 350°F.
2. Spray your air fryer tray with oil.
3. Drizzle pork chops with oil.
4. Season with onion powder, garlic powder and paprika.
5. Cook in the air fryer for 5 minutes per side.
6. Toss broccoli in avocado oil, garlic and salt.
7. Cook the broccoli in the air fryer for 3 minutes per side.

Serving Suggestion:

Sprinkle with pepper.

Tip:

You can use avocado oil instead of olive oil.

Pepper Pork Chops

Enjoy these succulent pork chops dotted with pepper.
Prep Time and Cooking Time: 10 minutes | Serves: 4

Ingredients to Use:

- 4 pork chops
- 2 to 3 teaspoons black pepper
- Cooking spray

Step-by-Step Directions

1. Start by flattening your pork on a cutting board.
2. Season with salt and pepper.
3. Cook at 320°F for 5 minutes per side.

Serving Suggestion:

Garnish with fresh herbs.

Tip:

Flatten pork chops with meat mallet before seasoning.

Parmesan Pork Fillet with Herbs

You'll love how Parmesan cheese and herbs come together to flavor up juicy pork fillet.
Prep Time and Cooking Time: 30 minutes | Serves: 4

Ingredients to Use:

- 4 pork chops
- Salt and pepper to taste
- 1/2 cup all-purpose flour
- 2 eggs
- 1/4 cup breadcrumbs
- 1/2 teaspoon garlic powder
- 1/4 cup Parmesan cheese, grated
- 1/2 teaspoon thyme
- 1/2 teaspoon oregano
- 1/2 teaspoon basil

- Cooking spray

Step-by-Step Directions

1. Sprinkle pork chops with salt and pepper.
2. Cover with flour.
3. Dip in eggs.
4. In a bowl, mix the remaining ingredients.
5. Dredge with breadcrumbs.
6. Spray with oil.
7. Cook at 360°F for 8 minutes
8. Turn and cook for another 8 minutes.

Serving Suggestion:

Serve with brown rice.

Tip:

Add a teaspoon of sugar to the herb mixture.

Crispy Pork Strips

Enjoy these golden crunchy pork strips seasoned with paprika and garlic.

Prep Time and Cooking Time: 20 minutes | Serves: 3

Ingredients to Use:

- 3 pork fillets, sliced into strips
- 2 teaspoons olive oil
- 1 teaspoon garlic powder
- 1 teaspoon paprika
- Salt and pepper to taste
- 1 egg
- 1 cup breadcrumbs

Step-by-Step Directions

1. Coat pork strips with oil.
2. Season with garlic powder, paprika, salt and pepper.
3. Dip in eggs.
4. Cover with breadcrumbs.
5. Cook at 350°F for 5 minutes per side.

Serving Suggestion:

Serve with dip of choice.

Tip:

Cook in batches so as not to overcrowd the air fryer.

Pork & Green Beans

Serve your crispy pork fillet with steamed green beans for a satisfying meal.

Prep Time and Cooking Time: 30 minutes | Serves: 4

Ingredients to Use:

- 1/4 cup almond flour
- 1 teaspoon Creole seasoning
- 1/4 cup Parmesan cheese, grated
- 1 teaspoon paprika
- 1 teaspoon garlic powder
- 4 pork chops
- 4 cups green beans, trimmed and steamed
- Cooking spray

Step-by-Step Directions

1. Preheat your air fryer to 375°F.
2. Spray your air fryer tray with oil.
3. In a bowl, mix all the ingredients except pork chops and green beans.
4. Spray pork chops with oil.
5. Coat with spice mixture.
6. Air fry for 15 minutes, turning once.

Serving Suggestion:

Serve with ketchup and hot sauce.

Tip:

You can also sprinkle green beans with Parmesan cheese before serving.

Pork & Potatoes

For sure, you're going to enjoy this beautiful pairing.

Prep Time and Cooking Time: 20 minutes | Serves: 2

Ingredients to Use:

- 2 pork chops
- 1 tablespoons oil
- 1 tablespoons steak seasoning
- 1 teaspoon paprika
- 2 cups French fries, cooked

Step-by-Step Directions

1. Preheat your air fryer to 400°F for 5 minutes.
2. Brush pork chops with oil.
3. Season with steak seasoning and paprika.
4. Air fry for 6 to 8 minutes per side.
5. Serve with French fries.

Serving Suggestion:

Garnish with lemon wedges and chopped scallions.

Tip:

Use pork chops that are at least 1 ½ inch thick.

Pork & Mushroom Bites

Delicious and easy to make—these pork and mushroom bites will be the star on the dinner table.

Prep Time and Cooking Time: 30 minutes | Serves: 4

Ingredients to Use:

- 1 lb. pork fillet, sliced into cubes
- 8 oz. mushrooms
- 1 teaspoon Worcestershire sauce
- 2 tablespoons butter, melted
- 1/2 teaspoon garlic powder
- Salt and pepper to taste

Step-by-Step Directions

1. Preheat your air fryer to 400°F for 5 minutes.
2. Toss all the ingredients in a bowl.
3. Transfer to the air fryer tray.
4. Cook at 400°F for 20 minutes, turning twice.

Serving Suggestion:

Serve with dip of choice.

Tip:

Extend cooking time if you want your pork more well done.

Pork & Brussels Sprouts

Serve your beautifully cooked with roasted Brussels sprouts.

Prep Time and Cooking Time: 30 minutes | Serves: 8

Ingredients to Use:

- 8 pork chops
- Cooking spray
- Salt and pepper to taste
- 1 teaspoon olive oil
- 1 teaspoon mustard
- 1 teaspoon maple syrup
- 6 oz. Brussels sprouts, sliced

Step-by-Step Directions

1. Spray your pork chops with oil.
2. Season with salt and pepper.
3. In a bowl, mix the remaining ingredients.
4. Add pork chops to the air fryer.
5. Cook for 5 minutes per side.
6. Transfer to a plate.
7. Add Brussels sprouts to the air fryer.
8. Cook for 3 minutes.

Serving Suggestion:

Season with pepper before serving.

Tip:

Use Dijon style mustard.

Pork with Mashed Potatoes

This dish will make you feel like you're in a top-rated restaurant.

Prep Time and Cooking Time: 25 minutes |

Serves: 4

Ingredients to Use:

- 4 pork chops
- Salt to taste
- 1 tablespoons mustard
- 1 egg, beaten
- 1 cup breadcrumbs
- 1/2 teaspoon onion powder
- 1/2 teaspoon garlic powder
- 1/4 cup Parmesan cheese, grated
- Cooking spray
- Cooked mashed potatoes

Step-by-Step Directions

1. Preheat your air fryer to 400°F for 10 minutes.
2. Season your pork chops with salt.
3. Mix the mustard and egg.
4. Dip pork chops in mustard mixture.
5. In another bowl, mix the remaining ingredients.
6. Dredge pork chops with breadcrumb mixture.
7. Spray with oil.
8. Cook in the air fryer for 6 minutes per side.
9. Serve with mashed potatoes.

Serving Suggestion:

Serve with steamed green beans.

Tip:

Season pork and mashed potatoes with pepper.

Honey Soy Pork Chops

You're going to enjoy every bite of this honey soy pork chops.

Prep Time and Cooking Time: 2 hours and 20 minutes | Serves: 4

Ingredients to Use:

- 1/2 cup soy sauce
- 1/4 cup honey
- Red pepper flakes
- 2 cloves garlic, minced
- 4 pork chops

Step-by-Step Directions

1. Combine soy sauce, honey, red pepper flakes and garlic in a bowl.
2. Soak the pork chops in the marinade.
3. Cover and refrigerate for 2 hours.
4. Choose grill setting in your air fryer oven.
5. Set it to medium high heat.
6. Cook for 8 to 10 minutes per side.

Serving Suggestion:

Let rest for 5 minutes before serving.

Tip:

Use low-sodium soy sauce.

Lemon Pepper Pork Chops

Serve delicious and juicy pork chops marinated in sauce with lemon pepper and garlic.

Prep Time and Cooking Time: 2 hours and 15 minutes | Serves: 6

Ingredients to Use:

- 2 cloves garlic, minced
- 1/4 cup soy sauce
- 1/2 cup water
- 3 tablespoons lemon pepper seasoning
- 1/4 cup vegetable oil
- 6 pork chops, fat trimmed

Step-by-Step Directions

1. Mix the garlic, soy sauce, water, lemon pepper seasoning and vegetable oil in a bowl.
2. Coat the pork chops with the sauce.
3. Marinate the pork chops in the sauce for 2 hours.
4. Choose grill setting in the air fryer oven.
5. Add the pork chops inside the air fryer

oven.

6. Grill the pork chops for 6 minutes per side.

Serving Suggestion:

Serve with roasted vegetables.

Tip:

Internal temperature should be 145°F.

Pork with Honey & Cumin

Flavor up your pork chops with honey, cumin and other spices.

Prep Time and Cooking Time: 1 hour and 20 minutes | Serves: 4

Ingredients to Use:

- 2 tablespoons vegetable oil
- 1 tablespoon apple cider vinegar
- 1/4 cup honey
- 1/2 teaspoon red pepper flakes
- 1 teaspoon ground cumin
- Salt and pepper to taste
- 8 pork chops

Step-by-Step Directions

1. Combine all the ingredients except pork chops in a bowl.
2. Add the pork chops to the bowl.
3. Cover and marinate in the refrigerator for 1 hour.
4. Preheat your air fryer oven to medium.
5. Set it to grill.
6. Cook the pork chops for 4 to 5 minutes per side.

Serving Suggestion:

Serve with tomato and cucumber salad.

Tip:

You can also increase temperature to sear the pork and give it grill marks.

Baked Pork & Veggies in Packets

Bake pork chops and vegetables in foil packets in the air fryer oven.

Prep Time and Cooking Time: 30 minutes | Serves: 4

Ingredients to Use:

- 4 pork chops
- Salt and pepper to taste
- 2 tablespoons canola oil
- 1 lb. potatoes, sliced into cubes
- 1 lb. asparagus, trimmed
- 1/2 lb. carrots, sliced into strips

Marinade

- 1 clove garlic, minced
- 1-1/2 teaspoons thyme, minced
- 1 tablespoon Creole seasoning
- 1 teaspoon Worcestershire sauce
- 3 tablespoons brown sugar
- 1/2 tablespoon Dijon-style mustard

Step-by-Step Directions

1. Select bake setting in your air fryer oven.
2. Season pork chops with salt and pepper.
3. In a bowl, mix the marinade ingredients.
4. Soak the pork chops in the marinade.
5. Cover and marinate for 2 hours.
6. In another bowl, toss the veggies in oil, salt and pepper.
7. Add the pork and veggies on top of a foil sheet.
8. Fold to make a packet.
9. Add to the air fryer oven.
10. Cook for 30 to 40 minutes.

Serving Suggestion:

Garnish with chopped parsley.

Tip:

Use bone-in pork chops that are at least ¾ inch thick.

Pork Rolls

Pork rolls are versatile enough to be served as a main course, appetizer or snack.

Prep Time and Cooking Time: 30 minutes | Serves: 6

Ingredients to Use:

- 1 onion, chopped
- 1 carrot, grated
- 1 green onion, minced
- 2 lb. ground pork
- 1 egg, beaten
- 12 egg roll wrappers
- Cooking spray

Step-by-Step Directions

1. Mix all the ingredients in a bowl except wrappers.
2. Top the wrappers with the pork mixture.
3. Roll and seal the wrappers.
4. Spray your rolls with oil.
5. Place the rolls in the air fryer oven.
6. Set it to air fry.
7. Cook at 370°F for 5 minutes.
8. Flip and cook for another 5 minutes.

Serving Suggestion:

Serve with sweet chili sauce.

Tip:

Use lean ground pork.

Mustard Pork Chop

Flavor up your pork chops with mustard and spices.

Prep Time and Cooking Time: 10 minutes | Serves: 4

Ingredients to Use:

- 4 pork chops
- 4 tablespoons mustard
- 1 teaspoon dried sage
- Salt and pepper to taste

Step-by-Step Directions

1. Spread mustard on both sides of pork chops.
2. Sprinkle with sage, salt and pepper.
3. Place the pork chops in the air fryer oven.
4. Set it to grill.
5. Cook at 320°F for 5 to 7 minutes per side.

Serving Suggestion:

Garnish with lemon wedges.

Tip:

Make sure that the pork's internal temperature is 145°F.

Maple Pork Sausage

These are savory and with just the right amount of sweet. For sure, you'll be delighted with this maple pork sausage recipe.

Prep Time and Cooking Time: 20 minutes | Serves: 6

Ingredients to Use:

- 2 lb. pork sausages
- 1/2 cup maple syrup
- 1 teaspoon dried sage
- 1 teaspoon dried thyme
- Salt and pepper to taste

Step-by-Step Directions

1. Coat the pork sausages with maple syrup.
2. Sprinkle with sage, thyme, salt and pepper.
3. Transfer to the air fryer oven.
4. Choose bake setting.
5. Cook at 400°F for 5 minutes.
6. Turn and cook for another 5 minutes.

Serving Suggestion:

Sprinkle with chopped parsley.

Tip:

Cook longer to make sure sausages are fully cooked.

Country-Style Fried Pork

This is the comfort food that you'll never get tired of.

Prep Time and Cooking Time: 15 minutes | Serves: 6

Ingredients to Use:

- 6 pork chops
- Salt and pepper to taste
- 1 teaspoon dried thyme
- 1 teaspoon dried oregano
- 1 cup flour
- 1 egg, beaten
- 1 cup bread crumbs
- Cooking spray

Step-by-Step Directions

1. Season pork with salt and pepper.
2. Sprinkle with thyme and oregano.
3. Cover with flour.
4. Dip in egg.
5. Dredge with breadcrumbs.
6. Spray with oil.
7. Place the pork chops in the air crisper tray.
8. Set the air fryer oven to air fry.
9. Cook at 400°F for 3 to 4 minutes per side.

Serving Suggestion:

Serve with fries.

Tip:

Dry the pork with paper towel before seasoning.

Italian Sausage Bites

You will fall in love with this crispy snack with origin Italian flavor.

Prep Time and Cooking Time: 15 minutes | Serves: 4

Ingredients to Use:

- 1 lb. Italian sausage, sliced in 2 to 3
- 2 tablespoons olive oil
- Pinch Italian seasoning

Step-by-Step Directions

1. Insert toothpicks into the sausages.
2. Drizzle with oil.
3. Sprinkle with Italian seasoning.
4. Add to the air crisper tray.
5. Set the air fryer oven to roast.
6. Roast at 400°F for 5 minutes.
7. Flip and cook for another 2 to 3 minutes until sausages are fully cooked.

Serving Suggestion:

Serve with marinara dip.

Tip:

You can also use other sausages for this recipe.

Baked Pork with Potatoes

Whether it's a special occasion or just an ordinary day at home, this pork with potatoes will surely delight everyone.

Prep Time and Cooking Time: 40 minutes | Serves: 4

Ingredients to Use:

Rub

- 1 tablespoon olive oil
- 2 teaspoons vinegar
- 1 clove garlic, minced
- 2 tablespoons ketchup
- 1 teaspoon Worcestershire Sauce
- 2 tablespoons brown sugar
- 1 tablespoon soy sauce
- Pork & potatoes
- 4 pork chops
- 1 tablespoon olive oil
- Salt and pepper to taste

Step-by-Step Directions

1. Set your air fryer oven to bake.
2. Preheat it to 430°F.
3. Mix the rub ingredients.

4. Coat the pork with the rub.
5. Marinate for 30 minutes.
6. Toss the potatoes in the oil.
7. Season with salt and pepper.
8. Spread in the air fryer oven.
9. Place the pork on one side.
10. Cook for 15 minutes.
11. Set the oven to broil.
12. Cook for 10 minutes.

Serving Suggestion:

Garnish with chopped parsley.

Tip:

Use cider vinegar.

Grilled Pork Belly

Yes, you can make delicious grilled pork belly using air fryer oven. Here's how.
Prep Time and Cooking Time: 4 hours | Serves: 6

Ingredients to Use:

- 3 lb. pork belly, sliced
- Marinade
- 1 clove garlic, minced
- 1 tablespoon lemon juice
- 1/2 cup soy sauce
- 1/2 cup ketchup
- Pepper to taste

Step-by-Step Directions

1. Mix the marinade ingredients in a bowl.
2. Coat the pork belly with the marinade.
3. Soak in the marinade for 3 hours, covered in the refrigerator.
4. Add the pork belly to the air fryer oven.
5. Set it to grill.
6. Cook at 370°F for 15 minutes per side, basting with the marinade every few minutes.
7. Choose roast setting in your air fryer oven.
8. Increase temperature to 430°F.
9. Cook for 10 minutes.

Serving Suggestion:

Serve with pickled onion or cucumber.

Tip:

Use thick-cut pork belly.

Sweet Bacon Knots

Here's a different way of preparing your bacon.
Prep Time and Cooking Time: 15 minutes | Serves: 4

Ingredients to Use:

- 1 lb. bacon
- 1/4 cup maple syrup
- 1/4 cup brown sugar

Step-by-Step Directions

1. Tie the bacon into a knot.
2. Place in the air fryer oven.
3. Brush with the maple syrup and sprinkle with the brown sugar.
4. Choose air fry setting.
5. Cook at 350°F for 10 minutes, flipping once or twice.

Serving Suggestion:

Garnish with chopped parsley.

Tip:

You can also use honey instead of maple syrup.

Chapter 5: Lamb & Goat Dishes

Air Fried Lamb Meatballs with Pesto

Spicy air-fried meatballs with a hint of sweetness from the raisin pesto.

Prep Time and Cooking Time: 25 minutes | Serves: 4

Ingredients to Use:

- 1 lb. lamb, ground
- 2 cloves of garlic, 1 grated 1 whole
- 2 cups mint leaves
- 3 tablespoons raisins
- 1/4 teaspoon turmeric powder
- 1/2 teaspoon cumin, ground
- 1/2 cup Japanese breadcrumbs
- 1/4 teaspoon red pepper flakes, crushed
- 1 large egg
- 1/4 cup finely chopped parsley, plus 1/2 cup parsley with soft stems
- 2 tablespoons, plus ½ cup of olive oil
- 1/2 cup Greek yogurt
- Kosher salt to taste

Step-by-Step Directions

1. In a large bowl, combine breadcrumbs, egg, red pepper flakes, cumin, finely chopped parsley, grated garlic, turmeric, 2 tablespoons of oil, and salt.
2. Add lamb to the mixture and combine using your hand.
3. Form and shape into meatballs (about the size of a golf ball).
4. Arrange meatballs with even spaces in between.
5. Choose the air fry function.
6. Air fry for 8 minutes at 400°F.
7. Turn meatballs halfway through for even browning.
8. In a blender, puree raisin, mint, parsley with stems, 1/2 cup of oil, 1 garlic clove, and salt to taste.

Serving Suggestion:

Spread yogurt on the plate first, then the pesto. Add the meatballs on top.

Tip:

The pesto can be made ahead of time and stored in the fridge.

Grilled Rosemary Jerk Lamb Chops

An easy lamb recipe oozing with umami flavors.

Prep Time and Cooking Time: 4 hours 30 minutes | Serves: 6-8

Ingredients to Use:

- 2 lb. lamb loin chops
- 1-1/2 tablespoons soy sauce
- 7 cloves garlic
- 1/3 cup scallions
- 1 sprig rosemary
- 1/2 Scotch bonnet chili
- 1/2 teaspoon allspice
- 1 medium yellow onion, chopped
- Salt and pepper to taste

Step-by-Step Directions

1. To make the marinade, blend soy sauce, garlic, onion, scallions, rosemary, chili, and allspice until smooth.
2. Coat and massage lamb chops with marinade.
3. Cover and chill for 4 hours.
4. Choose the grill option.

Grill lamb at 400°F for 11 to 14 minutes.

Serving Suggestion:

Garnish with rosemary sprigs.

Tip:

Lamb can be marinated overnight.

Grilled Lamb Chops with Tzatziki Sauce

Garlicky lamb paired with a refreshing yogurt and dill sauce.
Prep Time and Cooking Time: 1 hour 6 minutes | Serves: 2

Ingredients to Use:

- 4 lamb loin chops
- 3 tablespoons olive oil
- 1/2 teaspoon red chili flakes
- 2 teaspoons, plus 1 tablespoon fresh lemon juice
- 2 teaspoons dried dill
- 8 cloves garlic, minced
- 3/4 cup plain Greek yogurt
- 1/2 cup cucumber, minced
- Kosher salt and pepper to taste

Step-by-Step Directions

1. To create tzatziki sauce, whisk yogurt, 2 cloves minced garlic, 1 teaspoon dill, 1 tablespoon lemon juice, cucumber, salt, and pepper. Cover and chill.
2. Combine the remaining dill, garlic, lemon juice, chili flakes, and oil in a bowl to create the marinade.
3. Season lamb with salt and pepper and place in a baking tray.
4. Coat lamb with the marinade and leave at room temperature for 1 hour.
5. Choose the grill function in your air fryer.
6. Grill lamb at 350°F for 4 to 6 minutes (medium-rare).

Serving Suggestion:

Spread tzatziki sauce on a platter and lay lamb chops on top.

Tip:

A simple fresh green salad goes well with this dish.

Spiced Lamb Chops with Ginger Soy Sauce

A fragrant lamb recipe with a delicious dipping sauce.
Prep Time and Cooking Time: 2 hours 45 minutes | Serves: 8

Ingredients to Use:

- 8 lamb rib chops
- 1/3 cup scallions, finely chopped
- 3 tablespoons shallot, minced
- 2 tablespoons cilantro, minced
- 2 tablespoons ginger, minced
- 2 tablespoons garlic, minced
- 3 tablespoons oyster sauce
- 1 tablespoon sugar
- 2 tablespoons light soy sauce
- Steamed Bok choy
- Salt and pepper to taste
- Red and yellow bell peppers, julienned
- Scallions, julienned

Step-by-Step Directions

1. Combine oyster sauce, soy sauce, oil, cilantro, sugar, garlic, shallot, and ginger.
2. Add lamb chops and marinate for 2 hours at room temperature.
3. Choose grill function in your air fryer.
4. Place lamb in tray and season with salt and pepper.
5. Grill chops at 400°F for 6 minutes.
6. Transfer to a platter and cover with foil.
7. Let sit for 10 minutes.
8. Pour marinade into the pan and cook for 8 minutes or until it is reduced to create

the sauce.

Serving Suggestion:

Arrange steamed Bok choy in the plate and put lamb over together with julienned peppers and scallion. Serve with the sauce from the marinade.

Tip:

To reduce preparation time, marinate the lamb overnight, and keep in the fridge.

Spicy Lamb with Lentils & Herbs

Easy to make and wonderfully fragrant, you'll find this to be one of your go-to lamb recipes.
Prep Time and Cooking Time: 35 minutes | Serves: 4

Ingredients to Use:

- 1/2 lb. ground lamb
- 2 garlic cloves, thinly sliced
- 1/2 teaspoon cumin seeds
- 3/4 cup plain Greek yogurt
- 1 teaspoon crushed red pepper flakes
- 1/2 cucumber, chopped
- 1/4 cup fresh parsley
- 1/2 cup fresh cilantro, chopped
- 1-1/2 cups French green lentils
- 1 tablespoon vegetable oil
- Kosher salt and pepper to taste
- Flatbread and lemon wedges

Step-by-Step Directions

1. Season lamb with salt and pepper.
2. Place lamb on the baking sheet.
3. Choose the air fry option.
4. Air fry for 350°F for 5 minutes.
5. Break apart lamb and add red pepper flakes, cumin, and garlic.
6. Cook for 2 more minutes and set aside.
7. Season lentils with salt and pepper.
8. Put lentils in the baking pan and cook until brown for 6 minutes.
9. Add the lamb back and mix well.
10. Remove from heat and add parsley, cucumber, and cilantro.

Serving Suggestion:

Spread yogurt on the plate and put the lamb on top. Serve with the flatbread and lemon wedges.

Tip:

Garnish with fresh parsley and cilantro leaves.

Salt & Pepper Lamb

Simple yet delectable, this lamb recipe is also great as an appetizer.
Prep Time and Cooking Time: 45 minutes | Serves: 4

Ingredients to Use:

- 1-1/2 lb. lamb rump
- 4 oz. rice flour
- 3-1/2 oz. plain flour
- 3 egg whites
- 2 zucchinis, thinly sliced
- 1 red capsicum, sliced into strips
- 1 green capsicum, sliced into strips

Step-by-Step Directions

1. Cut lamb across the grain into thin strips.
2. Combine flours in a bowl and season with salt and pepper.
3. Whisk eggs in a separate bowl.
4. Dip strips of lamb in the egg then onto the flour individually.
5. Lightly coat a baking tray with oil.
6. Select the air fry option.
7. Air fry lamb for 3 to 4 minutes at 350°F.
8. Set aside lamb.
9. In the same tray, arrange the capsicums and zucchinis.
10. Air fry for 2 to 3 minutes until tender and

has light charring.

Serving Suggestion:

Serve lamb with charred vegetables, lime wedges, and mayonnaise

Tip:

You can also add freshly chopped onions as garnish.

Barbecue Lamb Cutlets

Try this easy air fryer barbecue at your next family dinner.
Prep Time and Cooking Time: 1 hour 10 minutes | Serves: 4

Ingredients to Use:

- 2 cups tomato ketchup
- 1/2 cup white vinegar
- 2 teaspoons Tabasco sauce
- 3 teaspoons Worcestershire sauce
- 1/2 cup brown sugar
- 1 onion, finely chopped
- 2 teaspoons mild mustard
- 4 large potatoes, cut into wedges
- 3-1/2 oz. sour cream
- 3 tablespoons vegetable oil
- 2 tablespoons mint, chopped
- Salt and pepper to taste
- 16 small lamb chops

Step-by-Step Directions

1. To make the marinade, combine onion, ketchup, vinegar, Worcestershire sauce, tabasco sauce, and sugar.
2. Soak lamb cuts in the marinade for 1 hour in the refrigerator.
3. Mix oil with salt and pepper.
4. Coat potatoes with the oil mixture.
5. Choose the air fry option.
6. Air fry at 400°F for 25 minutes until crispy.
7. Set aside potatoes once cooked.
8. Take out lamb and place it in the baking tray.
9. Air fry for 15 minutes at 350°F.

Serving Suggestion:

Place 4 pieces of lamb on each plate. Serve with potato wedged topped with sour cream and garnished with mint leaves.

Tip:

You can marinate the lamb overnight to save time.

Lamb Chops with Fresh Tomato Salad

A flavorful and well-balanced lamb dish that takes less than 20 minutes to make.
Prep Time and Cooking Time: 18 minutes | Serves: 1

Ingredients to Use:

- 1/4 teaspoon cinnamon, ground
- 2 tablespoons olive oil
- 2 lamb loin chops
- 1 tablespoon roasted pistachios, powdered
- 1 tablespoon white sesame seeds, toasted
- 1/2 lemon
- 4 scallions, thinly sliced
- 2 medium heirloom tomatoes, coarsely chopped
- 1 head little gem lettuce
- Kosher salt and pepper to taste

Step-by-Step Directions

1. Season lamb with salt then with cinnamon.
2. Lightly coat a baking tray with oil.
3. Select the air fry function.
4. Air fry lamb at 350°F for 3 minutes per side until brown.
5. Remove from heat and let rest for 5

minutes.
6. Set aside 2 tablespoons of pan drippings.
7. Pour the remaining drippings over the lamb.
8. In a bowl, toss together1 pinch of pistachio powder, sesame seeds, pepper, lemon zest, lemon juice, lettuce, tomatoes, and salt.

Serving Suggestion:

Arrange salad beside the lamb chops and sprinkle a generous amount of pistachio powder.

Tip:

You can substitute endive for the little gem lettuce. Adjust the cooking time if you like a little more done chop.

Air Fryer Marinated Lamb Chops

The wonderfully rendered fat and the spice marinade enhances the flavors in this must-try lamb dish.
Prep Time and Cooking Time: 3 hours 20 minutes | Serves: 4

Ingredients to Use:

- 12 lamb rib chops, frenched
- 1 teaspoon dried fenugreek leaves
- 1/2 teaspoon nutmeg, finely grated
- 1 teaspoon paprika
- 1/4 cup sour cream
- 1 serrano chile, finely grated
- 4 garlic cloves, finely grated
- 1 2-inch ginger, peeled and grated
- 1/2 teaspoon fennel seeds, toasted and ground
- 2 tablespoons fresh lime juice
- 2 tablespoons vegetable oil
- Kosher salt and pepper to taste

Step-by-Step Directions

1. In a bowl, combine sour cream, fennel powder, garlic, ginger, chile, fenugreek leaves, lime juice, pepper, nutmeg, paprika, and vegetable oil. Mix well.
2. Season lamb with salt and coat with spiced marinade.
3. Cover and chill in the refrigerator for 2 hours.
4. Remove from the refrigerator and let sit at room temperature at least 1 hour before grilling.
5. Lightly coat a baking tray with oil.
6. Select the grill function in your air fryer oven.
7. Grill each side for 3 minutes at 350°F for medium-rare.
8. Transfer to a plate and let rest for 10 minutes before serving.

Serving Suggestion:

Place 3 pieces of lamb chops on each plate. Dust chili or paprika powder over the lamb and serve with lemon wedges. Garnish with mint and cilantro.

Tip:

Adjust grilling time for the desired doneness. To cut on the preparation time, marinate the lamb overnight, and keep in the fridge.

Braised Lamb with Orange& Fennel

A lovely Mediterranean-inspired lamb dish that has exquisite flavors.
Prep Time and Cooking Time: 2 hours 7 minutes | Serves: 8

Ingredients to Use:

- 2 bay leaves
- 2 tablespoons olive oil
- 3 lb. boneless lamb shoulder, divided

into 8 pieces

- 1 garlic head, cut crosswise
- 1 medium onion, coarsely chopped
- 1 cinnamon stick
- 1 fennel bulb, coarsely chopped
- 1 can (14.5 oz.) peeled whole tomatoes
- 3 cups low-sodium chicken broth
- 1 cup dry white wine
- 1 whole orange, cut into pieces with the skin on

Step-by-Step Directions

1. Dry lamb pieces with paper towels.
2. Season with salt and pepper.
3. Lightly coat pot with oil.
4. Choose the grill function in your air fryer.
5. Grill lamb at 325°F for 6-8 minutes turning occasionally.
6. Transfer lamb to a plate.
7. Put garlic, onion, and fennel in the same pot and use the same settings.
8. Stir occasionally until golden brown for 6 minutes.
9. Deglaze the pot by adding wine.
10. Decrease temperature to 280°F.
11. Add cinnamon stick, orange, bay leaves, broth, tomatoes, and lamb.
12. Switch to bake function.
13. Cover with foil and bake for 1-1/2 hours at 280°F or until lamb is tender.
14. Transfer lamb to a plate and strain liquid through a sieve.
15. Pour the strained liquid back into the cooking pot and cook for 20 minutes until it achieves a velvety texture.
16. Put the lamb back in the cooking pot and coat lamb pieces with the sauce thoroughly.

Serving Suggestion:

This dish goes well with three-herb and onion salad, cucumber-dill tzatziki, or westward pita bread.

Tip:

You can add 2 tablespoons of pomegranate molasses towards the end.

Air Fryer Spiced Lamb Burger

This is a new take on an old favorite. This unique burger has a crunchy crust and is filled with vibrant flavors and aroma.
Prep Time and Cooking Time: 1 hour 15 minutes | Serves: 8

Ingredients to Use:

- 8 thick pita breads, with pockets
- 1/2 teaspoon ground cinnamon
- 1 tablespoon ground coriander
- 1 medium onion, finely chopped
- 3/4 cup fresh parsley, chopped
- 3/4 teaspoon ground cumin
- 1/4 cup olive oil
- 2-1/2 lb. ground lamb
- Kosher salt and pepper to taste

Step-by-Step Directions

1. In a large bowl, combine olive oil, lamb, pepper, parsley, salt, coriander, cinnamon, cumin, and onion.
2. Mix well using a fork.
3. Cover and chill for 1 hour.
4. Cut an opening on each pita bread and insert the lamb mixture.
5. Lightly press down along the opening of the pita to seal.
6. Lightly coat tray with oil.
7. Select the Air fry function in your air fryer oven.
8. Set temperature at 350°F.
9. Air fry pita bread for 5 minutes on each side.

Serving Suggestion:

Cut pita into halves or quarters.

Tip:

The filling can be made in advance and chilled in the fridge for 8 hours. You can also add cheese to the filling.

Air Fryer Barbecue Goat with Aubergine Sauce

The barbecued goat, tangy fresh dressing, and creamy sauce strikes the balance for a delish meal.

Prep Time and Cooking Time: 50 minutes | Serves: 2

Ingredients to Use:

- 1/2 teaspoon cinnamon powder
- 1 tablespoon cumin powder
- 1/2 tablespoon fennel seeds, ground
- 1/2 teaspoon of clove powder
- 1/4 teaspoon cardamom powder
- 1 tablespoon coriander powder
- 8 goat chops
- 4 tablespoons yogurt
- 1/4 cup lemon juice
- 2 aubergines
- 1 garlic head
- 1 teaspoon grape vinegar
- 1 teaspoon sumac
- 1 teaspoon pomegranate molasses
- Salt and pepper to taste

Step-by-Step Directions

1. Combine salt, pepper, fennel, cumin, coriander, cardamom, cinnamon, and clove powder in a bowl.
2. Massage the spice mixture to the goat meat and leave at room temperature for 30 minutes.
3. Choose the grill function.
4. Grill aubergines at 400°F for 10 minutes until the skin turns black and starts to break.
5. Add the whole head of garlic halfway.
6. Set aside aubergines and garlic to cool.
7. Once cool, peel off the skin and combine the aubergine and garlic in a bowl together with the lemon juice, yogurt, and salt. Mix well.
8. In a separate bowl, mix the grape vinegar, sumac, and pomegranate molasses with a teaspoon of boiling water.
9. Cook the goat chops using the same settings for 5 minutes on each side.

Serving Suggestion:

Serve goat on top of the flatbread with the aubergine sauce as a side dish. Drizzle the pomegranate dressing over the meat and aubergines.

Tip:

This dish goes well with a simple fresh herb salad.

Curried Chevon Stew

A scrumptious African and Caribbean dish that's perfectly spiced.

Prep Time and Cooking Time: 1 hour 45 minutes | Serves: 5

Ingredients to Use:

- 1 teaspoon garlic, minced
- 1 medium onion, sliced
- 2 tablespoons parsley, chopped
- 1 teaspoon smoked paprika
- 1 teaspoon ginger, minced
- 1 tablespoon bullion
- 1 teaspoon fresh thyme, chopped
- 2-1/2 lb. goat meat, cubed
- 1/2 cup cooking oil
- 3 teaspoons curry powder
- 2 green onions, sliced
- 4 tomatoes, diced
- 1 scotch bonnet pepper, chopped
- 2 cups stock
- Salt and pepper to taste

Step-by-Step Directions

1. Put goat meat in a pot.
2. Add water, salt, pepper, and some of the chopped onions
3. Choose the bake function.
4. Cook at 400°F for 1 hour until the goat is tender.
5. Remove the liquid and add oil.
6. Fry meat for 8 minutes until brown.
7. Add garlic, ginger, and the remaining onions and cook for 2 minutes.
8. Next add the paprika, parsley, curry powder, thyme, hot pepper, and diced tomatoes.
9. Stir frequently to prevent sticking.
10. Add stock, bullion, salt, and pepper. Mix.
11. Cover pot with foil and cook for 30 minutes. Add more water as needed to achieve the desired consistency.

Serving Suggestion:

Serve while hot together with white rice.

Tip:

Add green onions a few minutes before serving.

Spicy Roast Goat

A Nigerian goat dish filled with bold, smoky, and spicy flavors.

Prep Time and Cooking Time: 1 hour 30 minutes | Serves: 5

Ingredients to Use:

- 1 cup of onion, chopped
- 2 green onions, chopped
- 1 teaspoon ginger, minced
- 2 large tomatoes, chopped
- 2-1/2 lb. goat meat, cubed
- 3 cups or more water
- 1-1/2 tablespoons beef or chicken bouillon powder
- 3 tablespoons cooking oil
- 1 teaspoon smoked paprika
- 1/2 teaspoon curry powder
- 1 red or green bell pepper, chopped
- 2 or more scotch bonnet pepper
- 2 teaspoons garlic, minced
- Salt and white pepper to taste

Step-by-Step Directions

1. In a pot, mix goat, water, 1/2 tablespoon bouillon powder, salt, pepper, and some chopped onions.
2. Select the bake function and set the temperature to 400°F.
3. Cook goat meat until tender for 1 hour.
4. With a slotted spoon, transfer goat meat to a baking tray lined with foil.
5. Select the broil function.
6. Broil goat for 10 minutes turning halfway until brown. Set aside.
7. Add some cooking oil to the tray.
8. Put remaining chopped onion, ginger, and garlic.
9. After 1 minute, add green onion, paprika, curry powder, tomatoes, scotch bonnet, white pepper, and 1 tablespoon bouillon powder.
10. Cook for 7 minutes.
11. Add broiled goat and bell peppers and cook for 3 more minutes. Stirring occasionally.

Serving Suggestion:

Serve immediately after cooking.

Tip:

Can be paired with white rice or fried plantains.

Merguez Goat Meatballs

This easy to make North-African dish can be a wonderful appetizer as well as a delicious main course.

Prep Time and Cooking Time: 45 minutes | Serves: 3

Ingredients to Use:

- 1/2 teaspoon coriander, ground
- 1 teaspoon paprika
- 1/2 cup onion, finely chopped
- 1/4 teaspoon cayenne
- 1/4 teaspoon fennel, ground
- 1/2 teaspoon cumin, ground
- 2 cloves garlic, minced
- 1 lb. ground goat meat
- 1 tablespoon harissa paste (Moroccan red pepper sauce)
- 1/2 cup plain Greek yogurt
- 1 tablespoon fresh basil, finely chopped
- 1/4 cup feta cheese, crumbled
- Kosher salt and ground black pepper to taste

Step-by-Step Directions

1. In a bowl, combine ground goat, onion, garlic, coriander, paprika, cayenne, fennel, cumin, salt, and pepper.
2. With clean hands, mix all the ingredients until spices are evenly distributed.
3. Line baking tray with parchment paper.
4. Roll goat meat into 3-inch long meatballs and arrange in the tray.
5. Select the bake function in your air fryer oven.
6. Bake meatballs at 400°F for 30 minutes until brown.
7. In a bowl, mix yogurt, basil, feta, salt, and pepper to create the yogurt sauce. Set aside.

Serving Suggestion:

Serve meatballs immediately and add a dollop of yogurt sauce on top.

Tip:

Remember to not overmix the ground meat since it can become tough. Can be served on top of couscous as a main dish or as party appetizers.

Goat in Creole Sauce

A popular Haitian dish that could be your new comfort food.

Prep Time and Cooking Time: 3 hours 35 minutes | Serves: 6-8

Ingredients to Use:

- 4 garlic cloves, grated
- 1 medium white onion, sliced
- 1/3 cup tomatoes, chopped
- 1 sprig fresh thyme, finely chopped
- 1/4 cup fresh parsley, finely chopped
- 1 tablespoon olive oil
- 3 whole cloves
- 2 scallions, chopped
- 1/2 green bell pepper, sliced
- 3 lb. goat meat, cubed
- 1 cup white vinegar or lemon juice
- 1/3 cup unsweetened orange juice
- 1 tablespoon tomato paste
- Salt and black pepper to taste

Step-by-Step Directions

1. Pour lemon juice or vinegar on goat meat and massage.
2. Rinse with cold water and drain.
3. In a bowl, combine all spices, orange juice, and goat meat.
4. Cover and chill for at least 2 hours.
5. Allow meat to attain room temperature before cooking.
6. Put goat meat in a pot and add water until the meat is covered.
7. Choose bake function.
8. Cook meat at 400°F for 1 hour or until tender.
9. Add water as needed.
10. With a slotted spoon, transfer meat to a plate and set aside.
11. Strain liquid and set aside.
12. Choose roast function and set to 350°F.
13. Add oil and tomato paste to the pot.

14. Add meat and cook for 5 minutes.
15. Add chopped tomatoes and cook for 2 minutes.
16. Add sauce gradually until desired consistency.
17. Add onion, bell pepper, salt, and pepper.
18. Cook for 7 minutes.

Serving Suggestion:

Serve with rice or any root vegetables.

Tip:

When adding water, use hot water. Cold water tends to make the meat taste bland.

Air Fryer Goat Steak

A garlic-infused goat steak recipe you can easily make in your air fryer at home.
Prep Time and Cooking Time: 2 hours 10 minutes | Serves: 2

Ingredients to Use:

- 4 garlic cloves, minced
- 2 tablespoons fresh oregano, chopped
- 1 cup sheep's milk yogurt
- Salt and pepper to taste
- 2 tablespoons oil
- 2 1-inch thick goat steaks

Step-by-Step Directions

1. Rub goat generously with salt and pepper.
2. Combine yogurt, oregano, and garlic in a small bowl.
3. Massage the yogurt mixture into the goat.
4. Cover and chill for 2 hours.
5. Lightly coat tray with oil.
6. Choose the air fry option.
7. Air fry goat steaks at 350°F for 2 minutes on each side.

Serving Suggestion:

Tent with foil for 5 minutes after cooking.

Tip:

Carefully watch the goat meat when frying, as it can dry out quickly. Goat steaks taste better when allowed to marinate at least overnight. Do this in advance to save time.

Ground Goat & Sweet Potatoes

A filling goat recipe with just the right amount of spice.
Prep Time and Cooking Time: 50 minutes | Serves: 4

Ingredients to Use:

- 1 tablespoon olive oil
- 1 clove garlic, minced
- 1/4 cup fresh cilantro, chopped
- 1 teaspoon coriander
- 2 lb. sweet potatoes, peeled and diced into 1/4-inch cubes
- 1 large onion, chopped
- 2 tablespoons lemon juice
- 1/4 teaspoon of garam masala
- 1 cup plain yogurt
- 1 lb. ground goat meat
- Salt to taste

Step-by-Step Directions

1. Add sweet potatoes to a pot and cover with water.
2. Choose bake function.
3. Bake for 400°F for 30 minutes until soft. Set aside.
4. Select the air fry function.
5. Air fry onion with some olive oil in a baking tray for 5 minutes until soft.
6. Add ground goat and cook until light brown.
7. Add the sweet potatoes, garam masala, cilantro, coriander, and salt.
8. Cook for 5 minutes at 350°F.
9. Combine yogurt, garlic, and lemon juice in a bowl to make the yogurt sauce.

Serving Suggestion:

Serve goat meat with a dollop of yogurt sauce on top.

Tip:

Gently stir to avoid breaking or mashing the sweet potatoes.

Chevon Lahmacun

A Turkish classic with a brilliant twist. This recipe swaps lamb for sustainable and tasty goat meat.
Prep Time and Cooking Time: 1 hour 30 minutes | Serves: 8

Ingredients to Use:

- 2 teaspoons dry yeast
- 1-3/4 teaspoon sugar
- 3 cups strong white bread flour, plus more for dusting
- 2 teaspoons salt
- 1 cup lukewarm water
- 2 tablespoons tomato puree
- Pepper to taste
- 5 tablespoons olive oil
- 1 lb. minced goat
- 1 red pepper, seeded and chopped
- 3 garlic cloves, chopped
- 1 white onion, chopped
- 1 pinch red pepper or chili flakes
- 1 bunch parsley, chopped

Step-by-Step Directions

1. In a large bowl, mix flour and salt.
2. Dissolve yeast in lukewarm water.
3. Add 3 tablespoons olive oil and 1-3/4 teaspoon sugar to the yeast water. Mix.
4. Gently pour the liquid into the bowl with flour.
5. Using hands, mix until you get a rough dough.
6. Take out the dough and knead until soft and elastic.
7. Place the dough back in the bowl. Dust with flour and cover with a towel.
8. Let the dough rise in a warm area for an hour.
9. Combine goat along with all other ingredients in a food processor until a smooth paste consistency is achieved.
10. Divide dough into 4-8 balls, depending on your preference.
11. Roll each dough ball flat and top with a generous amount of goat mixture.
12. Place dough on a baking tray.
13. Choose the
14. cook for 6-10 minutes.

Serving Suggestion:

Add parsley and a drizzle of pomegranate molasses on top.

Tip:

If the dough is too wet, you can add a little flour. If it's too dry, add a little water. The lahmacun is ready if the goat is sizzling and the edges have become brown.

Easy Air Fryer Goat Curry

This is the most popular way to prepare goat meat and for good reason.
Prep Time and Cooking Time: 1 hour 10 minutes | Serves: 4

Ingredients to Use:

- 10 garlic cloves, finely grated
- 1 onion, sliced
- 2 tablespoons chili powder
- 2 teaspoons curry leaves
- 2 lb. goat shoulder, cubed
- 2 cinnamon quills
- 5 tablespoons vegetable oil
- 1 teaspoon castor sugar
- 1 lemon, juiced
- 8 fl. coconut cream
- 17 oz. water

- 2 tablespoons fennel seeds, ground
- 1 oz. ginger

Step-by-Step Directions

1. In a small bowl, mix the garlic, fennel, and ginger into a paste.
2. Choose the bake option.
3. Coat pan with oil and put cinnamon quills, curry leaves, onions.
4. Cook for 5 minutes at 350°F.
5. Add the garlic, ginger, and fennel paste.
6. Add the goat and cook for 5 minutes until brown.
7. Add water and reduce temperature to 190°F.
8. Cook for 40 minutes.
9. Add the coconut milk, lemon juice, salt, and sugar.
10. Stir and continue cooking until liquids have evaporated.

Serving Suggestion:

Serve with a steamy bowl of rice.

Tip:

Garnish with fresh parsley.

Moorish Goat Skewers

Spicy and savory goat skewers ideal for any occasion.

Prep Time and Cooking Time: 6 hours 30 minutes | Serves: 4

Ingredients to Use:

- 1 teaspoon turmeric
- 2 oz. olive oil
- 2 garlic cloves, finely minced
- 1 teaspoon nutmeg, ground
- 1/2 teaspoon, plus 1/2 teaspoon cayenne pepper
- 1 bunch curly parsley, chopped
- 7 oz. fino, plus 2 oz. sherry
- 2 tablespoons cumin seeds, ground
- 1 tablespoon, plus 1 teaspoon sweet Spanish paprika
- 1/2 lemon, squeezed
- 2 lb. goat meat, cut into 1-inch cubes
- Salt to taste

Step-by-Step Directions

1. In a large bowl, mix cumin, nutmeg, turmeric, garlic, parsley, ½ teaspoon cayenne powder, 1 tablespoon paprika, 7 oz. fino, and olive oil.
2. Add goat meat.
3. Cover and chill for 6 hours or overnight.
4. Thread goat cubes into metal skewers.
5. To create basting liquid, mix 2 oz. sherry, 1/2 teaspoon cayenne pepper, 1 teaspoon paprika, and lemon juice.
6. Choose the grill or use the rotisserie function in your air fryer oven.
7. Set the temperature to 200°F and cook for 15 minutes.
8. Brush basting liquid occasionally.

Serving Suggestion:

Allow meat to rest for a few minutes before serving.

Tip:

While marinating, turn or stir 2-3 times to coat goat meat evenly. Make a big batch and store it in the fridge to easily cook anytime in your air fryer.

Kid Goat Ragu with Pappardelle

This Greek-inspired goat dish is brilliantly well-balanced and undeniably delicious.

Prep Time and Cooking Time: 1 hour 45 minutes | Serves: 4

Ingredients to Use:

- 1 garlic clove, sliced
- 2 onions, chopped
- 1 cup of water
- 4 celery sticks, chopped

- 2 oz. extra virgin olive oil
- 1 carrot, cubed
- 18 oz. white wine
- 1 teaspoon thyme leaves
- 2 bird's eye chilis, thinly sliced
- 1/2 cup pecorino
- 2 lb. kid goat shoulders, cut into 3 pieces each
- 2 lb. pappardelle pasta, cooked al dente
- Salt and freshly ground pepper to taste

Step-by-Step Directions

1. Put olive oil in the pot.
2. Add garlic, celery, carrots, and onions.
3. Select the air fryer option.
4. Cook the vegetables for 3 minutes at 200°F.
5. Increase temperature to 350°F.
6. And add the meat. Cook for 8 minutes until golden brown.
7. Add water, thyme, white wine, and season with salt and pepper.
8. Cover and cook for 90 minutes.
9. Shred meat and remove from bone.
10. Toss pasta with sauce.

Serving Suggestion:

Sprinkle pecorino over the goat and pasta.

Tip:

Top with sliced chili as a garnish.

Jamaican Goat Curry

This goat recipe is a delightful introduction to Jamaican cuisine.

Prep Time and Cooking Time: 2 hours 45 minutes | Serves: 6

Ingredients to Use:

- 2 teaspoons minced garlic
- 1 medium onion, sliced
- 2 scallions, sliced
- 1 tablespoon tomato paste
- 1 tablespoon bouillon powder
- 3 lb. goat meat, cut into chunks
- 1 scotch bonnet pepper
- 3 medium potatoes
- 1/4 cup cooking oil
- 2 teaspoons minced ginger
- 4 tablespoons curry powder
- 2 teaspoons fresh thyme
- Salt and white pepper to taste

Step-by-Step Directions

1. Generously rub goat meat with salt and pepper. Set aside.
2. Choose the air fry option.
3. Lightly coat pot with oil.
4. Air fry goat meat until brown.
5. Add curry powder and cook for 2 minutes.
6. Stir in tomato paste, scallions, garlic, onion, ginger, scotch bonnet, thyme, and white pepper.
7. Add hot water enough to cover the goat.
8. Cook for 1-1/2 to 2 hours until meat is tender.
9. Add hot water or stock as needed.
10. Add potatoes and bouillon powder cook for 20 minutes.

Serving Suggestion:

Serve hot in a bowl with rice or mashed potatoes.

Tip:

Garnish with fresh herbs and lime wedges.

Easy Air Fried Goat

This recipe has savory and tangy flavors that go so well with goat meat.

Prep Time and Cooking Time: 45 minutes | Serves: 4

Ingredients to Use:

- 2 teaspoons garlic, minced

- 1 teaspoon paprika
- 4 tablespoons lemon juice
- 2 lb. kid goat meat, cubed
- 2 tablespoons cooking oil

Step-by-Step Directions

1. Season goat meat with salt, lemon juice, paprika, and garlic.
2. Cover and rest for 30 minutes at room temperature.
3. Choose the air fry function.
4. Lightly coat a baking tray with oil.
5. Air fry goat at 400°F until brown.

Serving Suggestion:

Serve with fresh salad. Drizzle some more lemon juice before serving.

Tip:

For a spicy version, sprinkle with chili powder or hot sauce.

Goat with Rosemary & Bay Leaf

A traditional Zimbabwe goat dish with a pleasant twist.
Prep Time and Cooking Time: 1 hour 30 minutes | Serves: 5

Ingredients to Use:

- 3 garlic cloves, minced
- 2 lb. goat meat, cubed
- 2 sprigs fresh rosemary
- 2 tablespoons cooking oil
- 1 bay leaf
- Salt to taste

Step-by-Step Directions

1. Coat pot with oil.
2. Choose the grill function.
3. Put goat in pot and season with salt.
4. Grill goat until golden brown at 400°F.
5. Add bay leaf, rosemary, and garlic to the pot.
6. Add hot water enough to cover the meat.
7. Cook until liquid evaporates.
8. Brown goat again for 5 minutes.

Serving Suggestion:

Serve with sadzaregorosi (wheatmeal pap)

Tip:

Goes well with sadzanemuriwo (sautéed meat and vegetables) and soup.

Punjabi-style Goat Curry

This traditional Indian curry is easy to make and is full of great flavors and aroma.
Prep Time and Cooking Time: 1 hour 40 minutes | Serves: 6

Ingredients to Use:

- 4 cloves, crushed
- 1 tablespoon turmeric powder
- 2 teaspoon garam masala powder
- 1 tablespoon chili powder
- 2 teaspoon paprika powder
- 1 tablespoon coriander powder
- 2 green cardamoms, crushed
- 3 tablespoons ginger, chopped
- 1 bay leaf
- 1 cup olive oil
- 1 large yellow onion (crushed in a food processor)
- 2 cups canned tomato sauce
- 2 tablespoon fresh Indian chili, chopped
- 1 bunch fresh coriander leaves
- 9 cups hot water
- 3 lb. goat meat, cut into chunks
- Salt to taste

Step-by-Step Directions

1. Coat pot with oil.
2. Choose the bake or roast function.
3. Add cloves, onion, bay leaf, cumin, and cardamom.

4. Cook until onion turns light brown.
5. Add chili paste, garlic, and ginger.
6. Add goat and cook for 15 minutes.
7. Add chili powder, paprika, coriander, turmeric, tomato sauce, and salt. Mix well.
8. Once the oil starts to form, add the hot water, and continue stirring.
9. Add water as needed.
10. Cover with foil and continue baking until meat is fork-tender.

Serving Suggestion:

Add the garam masala and coriander leaves a few minutes before serving.

Tip:

This goes well with steamed rice and Indian bread.

Spiced Masala Chops

If you're someone trying out goat meat for the first time, this spice-infused recipe is perfect for you.

Prep Time and Cooking Time: 40 minutes | Serves: 3

Ingredients to Use:

- 1 tablespoon white vinegar
- 1 tablespoon turmeric powder
- 1/2 tablespoon garam masala
- 1 tablespoon cumin powder
- 1-1/2 Kashmiri red chili powder
- 2 tablespoon ginger and garlic paste
- 1 lb. goat chops
- 2 tablespoon cooking oil
- Salt to taste

Step-by-Step Directions

1. Coat pot with oil.
2. Choose the roast or bake function in your air fryer oven.
3. Set temperature at 350°F.
4. Add the garlic and ginger paste for a few seconds.
5. Put chops and cook until brown.
6. Put all remaining ingredients and add some water.
7. Add 1/2 cup of hot water and cook for 25 minutes until liquids evaporate.
8. Put chops in the air fryer basket.
9. Roast for 8-10 minutes at 356°F.

Serving Suggestion:

Serve with any yogurt dip and fresh salad.

Tip:

Goes well with steamed rice.

Chapter 6: Chicken & Poultry Dishes

Sweet & Sour Turkey

If you love sweet and sour chicken, for sure, you're going to enjoy this amazing dish that's very easy to do.
Prep Time and Cooking Time: 30 minutes | Serves: 4

Ingredients to Use:

- 1 lb. chicken breast fillet, trimmed and sliced
- 1/2 cup cornstarch
- Cooking spray

Sauce

- 4 tablespoons mayonnaise
- tablespoons sweet chili sauce
- 2 tablespoons vinegar
- 2 tablespoons chili garlic paste

Step-by-Step Directions

1. Coat the chicken slices with cornstarch.
2. Spray your chicken with oil.
3. Set your air fryer oven to air fry.
4. Cook at 400°F for 5 minutes.
5. Flip and cook for another 5 minutes.
6. Combine the ingredients for the sauce.
7. Toss the chicken in the sauce.
8. Put the chicken back to the air fryer oven.
9. Choose bake setting.
10. Bake at 400°F for 5 minutes.

Serving Suggestion:

Sprinkle with chopped scallions and roasted peanuts.

Tip:

Use rice vinegar.

Turkey with Artichoke

The crispy texture and delicious flavors will make you go wow with this dish.
Prep Time and Cooking Time: 30 minutes | Serves: 2

Ingredients to Use:

- 1/2 teaspoon poultry seasoning
- 1 tablespoon Italian seasoning
- 1 cup breadcrumbs
- 1/4 cup cheddar cheese, shredded
- 2 tablespoon cream cheese
- 2 tablespoons onions, minced
- 1 lb. turkey breast fillet
- 1/2 cup mayonnaise
- Cooking spray
- 1/4 cup tomatoes, diced
- oz. baby artichokes, sliced

Step-by-Step Directions

1. Mix the herbs and breadcrumbs in a bowl.
2. In another bowl, mix the cheddar cheese, cream cheese and onions.
3. Spread both sides of turkey with mayo.
4. Dredge with breadcrumb mixture.
5. Add these to the air crisper tray.
6. Spray the turkey with oil.
7. Select air fry option in your air fryer oven.
8. Cook at 370°F for 7 minutes.
9. Flip and cook for 5 minutes.
10. Spread the topping on top of the turkey.
11. Place the tomatoes and artichokes on top.
12. Choose roast option.
13. Cook at 350°F for 10 minutes.

Serving Suggestion:

Sprinkle with pepper and serve.

Tip:

Flatten the turkey with meat mallet.

Onion Turkey

You'll find yourself speechless once you get a taste of this amazing turkey dish.

Prep Time and Cooking Time: 30 minutes | Serves: 4

Ingredients to Use:

- 1/2 cup flour
- Salt and pepper to taste
- 1 egg
- 2 tablespoons mayonnaise
- 1 lb. turkey breast fillet
- 1 cup fried onions, crushed
- Cooking spray

Step-by-Step Directions

1. Mix flour, salt and pepper in a bowl.
2. In another bowl, beat the egg.
3. Stir in the mayo.
4. In the third bowl, add the dried onions.
5. Coat the turkey with the flour mixture, egg mixture and then with the crushed dried onions.
6. Spray with oil.
7. Arrange in a single layer in the air crisper tray.
8. Select air fry function.
9. Cook the turkey at 370°F for 6 minutes per side.

Serving Suggestion:

Serve with fresh green salad.

Tip:

Spray both sides evenly with oil to get a crispy texture.

Red Pepper Jelly Chicken Wings

You'll love the spicy flavor of these chicken wings. These are delicious, crispy and easy to make.

Prep Time and Cooking Time: 40 minutes | Serves: 6

Ingredients to Use:

- Salt to taste
- 3 tablespoons baking powder
- 1 lb. chicken wings
- Cooking spray
- 1 cup red pepper jelly

Step-by-Step Directions

1. Combine salt and baking powder in a bowl.
2. Coat chicken wings with the mixture.
3. Spray with oil.
4. Add to the air fryer oven.
5. Choose the air fry option.
6. Cook at 380°F for 15 minutes.
7. Flip and cook for another 10 minutes.
8. Heat the jelly in a pan over medium heat.
9. Toss the chicken in the jelly before serving.

Serving Suggestion:

Garnish with red pepper flakes or chopped green onion before serving.

Tip:

You can also use turkey wings for this recipe.

Turkey & Veggie Stir Fry

Here's a light and filling meal that you'd surely enjoy.

Prep Time and Cooking Time: 20 minutes | Serves: 4

Ingredients to Use:

- 1 tablespoon sesame oil
- 1 lb. turkey breast fillet, sliced into cubes
- 16 oz. frozen vegetables
- 1 clove garlic, minced
- 1 teaspoon Italian seasoning

Step-by-Step Directions

1. Coat turkey and veggies with sesame oil.
2. Sprinkle with garlic and Italian seasoning.
3. Choose air fry setting in your air fryer oven.
4. Cook the chicken at 370°F for 7 minutes.
5. Stir in the vegetables.
6. Cook for 5 minutes.

Serving Suggestion:

Garnish with chopped herbs.

Tip:

Thaw the vegetables first before air frying.

Chicken Piccata

A flavorful dish that will become a regular in your weekly menu.

Prep Time and Cooking Time: 30 minutes | Serves: 4

Ingredients to Use:

Chicken breasts

- 1 lb. chicken, sliced thinly
- Salt and pepper to taste
- 1 teaspoon garlic powder
- 1 tablespoon lemon juice
- 1 egg white, beaten
- 1/2 cup Italian bread crumbs
- Cooking spray

Piccata Sauce

- 1 tablespoon butter
- 3/4 cup chicken stock
- 2 tablespoons lemon juice
- Salt and pepper to taste

Step-by-Step Directions

1. Season chicken with salt and pepper.
2. In a bowl, combine the garlic powder, lemon juice and egg white.
3. In another bowl, add the breadcrumbs.
4. Dip the chicken in garlic powder mixture.
5. Dredge with breadcrumbs.
6. Spray both sides with oil.
7. Place chicken in the air crisper tray.
8. Cook at 350°F for 5 minutes.
9. In a pan over medium low heat, mix the butter, lemon juice and broth.
10. Season with salt and pepper.
11. Simmer for 5 minutes, stirring often.
12. Drizzle chicken with sauce and serve.

Serving Suggestion:

Garnish with capers.

Tip:

Be sure to trim the skin of chicken before cooking.

Balsamic Glazed Turkey

Be ready to fall head over heels in love with this savory balsamic glazed turkey.

Prep Time and Cooking Time: 30 minutes | Serves: 4

Ingredients to Use:

- 1 teaspoon garlic, minced
- 1/2 cup balsamic vinegar
- 4 tablespoons honey
- 1 teaspoon honey mustard
- Salt and pepper to taste
- 4 turkey thigh fillets

Step-by-Step Directions

1. Combine all the ingredients except turkey thigh fillets.
2. Add the turkey to an air fryer safe pan.
3. Place this inside the air fryer oven.
4. Pour the sauce over the turkey.
5. Select roast setting.
6. Cook at 350°F for 7 minutes per side.

Serving Suggestion:

Sprinkle with pepper before serving.

Tip:

If turkey is not fully cooked at 15 minutes, cook for 5 more minutes.

Lemon Garlic Turkey Kebab

These kebabs are always a big hit in parties!
Prep Time and Cooking Time: 8 hours and 30 minutes | Serves: 4

Ingredients to Use:

- 1 lb. turkey breast fillets, sliced into cubes
- 1 bell pepper, sliced
- 1 onion, sliced

Marinade

- 3 tablespoons lemon juice
- 1/4 cup olive oil
- 2 cloves garlic, minced
- Salt and pepper to taste

Step-by-Step Directions

1. Combine the marinade ingredients in a bowl.
2. Divide into 2 bowl.
3. Marinate turkey cubes in the first bowl.
4. Marinate vegetables in the second bowl.
5. Cover and refrigerate for 8 hours.
6. Thread the turkey and vegetables onto skewers.
7. Add to the air crisper tray.
8. Choose grill setting.
9. Cook at 350°F for 5 minutes per side.

Serving Suggestion:

Garnish with lemon wedges.

Tip:

You can also separate a small amount of sauce for basting.

Barbecue Turkey Fillets

Turkey fillets drenched in sweet savory barbecue sauce is truly delightful.
Prep Time and Cooking Time: 30 minutes | Serves: 4

Ingredients to Use:

- 1 lb. turkey fillets, sliced
- Cooking spray
- Salt and pepper
- 1/2 cup barbecue sauce, divided

Step-by-Step Directions

1. Spray turkey with oil.
2. Sprinkle both sides of turkey with salt and pepper.
3. Brush with half of the barbecue sauce.
4. Add to the air fryer oven.
5. Select bake setting.
6. Cook at 350°F for 10 minutes per side.
7. Toss in the barbecue sauce.
8. Cook for another 5 minutes.

Serving Suggestion:

Garnish with chopped onions.

Tip:

You can also make your own barbecue sauce by mixing ketchup, honey, soy sauce, lemon juice and pepper.

Caribbean Chicken

Here's a recipe that's friendly in terms of both cost and time.
Prep Time and Cooking Time: 15 minutes | Serves: 4

Ingredients to Use:

- 4 chicken thighs
- Cooking spray

Seasoning

- 2 teaspoons cayenne pepper
- 1 teaspoon dried thyme
- 1 teaspoon dried basil
- 2 teaspoons paprika
- Salt and pepper to taste

Step-by-Step Directions

1. Combine all the seasoning ingredients.
2. Sprinkle both sides of chicken with this mixture.

3. Transfer chicken to the air fryer oven.
4. Select roast function.
5. Cook at 350°F for 10 minutes per side.
6. Spray with oil.
7. Put the chicken back to the air fryer.
8. Choose air fry setting.
9. Cook at 350°F for 5 minutes.

Serving Suggestion:

Garnish with lemon wedges.

Tip:

Remove skin of chicken before seasoning and cooking.

Orange Turkey

Here's a unique twist to orange chicken that you'll enjoy. This one uses turkey fillets instead of chicken.

Prep Time and Cooking Time: 30 minutes | Serves: 2

Ingredients to Use:

- 2 turkey breast fillets, diced
- Salt and pepper to taste
- 1/2 cup flour
- 1 teaspoon butter
- 3 tablespoons orange juice
- 2 teaspoons orange zest
- 1 teaspoon honey

Step-by-Step Directions

1. Season turkey breast slices with salt and pepper.
2. Cover with flour.
3. Add to the air fryer tray.
4. Set it to air fry.
5. Cook at 370°F for 10 minutes.
6. Flip and cook for another 7 minutes.
7. Add butter to a pan over medium heat.
8. Once melted, add the orange juice, orange zest and honey.
9. Simmer while stirring for 1 minute.
10. Toss the turkey slices in the mixture.
11. Put them back to the air fryer oven.
12. Select bake function.
13. Cook at 350°F for 2 minutes.

Serving Suggestion:

Garnish with orange slices.

Tip:

You can also add herbs to the breading if you like.

Grilled Herb Chicken

Simple but satisfying—there are so many wonderful words to describe this grilled herb chicken.

Prep Time and Cooking Time: 1 hour and 30 minutes | Serves: 2

Ingredients to Use:

- 2 chicken breast fillets

Marinade

- 1/4 cup olive oil
- 2 cloves garlic, minced
- 1 teaspoon orange zest
- 1 teaspoon lemon zest
- 1 teaspoon dried thyme
- 1 teaspoon dried oregano
- 1 teaspoon dried basil
- Salt and pepper to taste

Step-by-Step Directions

1. Mix marinade ingredients in a bowl.
2. Add the chicken to the bowl.
3. Cover and marinate for 1 hour.
4. Add chicken to the air fryer oven.
5. Select grill setting.
6. Cook at 350°F for 7 minutes per side.
7. Increase temperature to 400°F.
8. Cook for another 6 minutes.

Serving Suggestion:

Garnish with grilled onion slices and lemon

wedges.

Tip:

You can also use fresh herbs if you like.

Spiced Turkey

This is another irresistible turkey recipe that you shouldn't take long to try.

Prep Time and Cooking Time: 20 minutes | Serves: 4

Ingredients to Use:

- 4 turkey breast fillets
- 4 tablespoons olive oil
- Salt and pepper to taste
- teaspoons harissa paste

Step-by-Step Directions

1. Brush turkey with olive oil.
2. Season both sides with salt, pepper and harissa paste.
3. Place the turkey inside the air fryer oven.
4. Select air fry option.
5. Cook at 370°F for 7 minutes per side.

Serving Suggestion:

Serve on top of vegetable salad.

Tip:

Dry the chicken thoroughly before seasoning.

Turkey with Creamy Lemon Sauce

With this recipe, you don't have to beat yourself up coming up with something fancy and special.

Prep Time and Cooking Time: 20 minutes | Serves: 4

Ingredients to Use:

- 4 turkey breast fillets
- Salt and pepper to taste
- 1 tablespoon olive oil, divided

Sauce

- 2 tablespoons butter
- 1 cup red onion, minced
- 3 tablespoons garlic, minced
- 1 cup chicken broth
- 1 tablespoon lemon juice
- 1/4 cup heavy cream
- 1 teaspoon fresh dill, minced

Step-by-Step Directions

1. Season the turkey with salt and pepper.
2. Drizzle with half of the oil.
3. Toss the onion slices in the remaining oil.
4. Place the turkey and onion slices in the air fryer oven.
5. Set the air fryer oven to air fry.
6. Cook at 370°F for 7 minutes per side.
7. Add the butter to a pan over medium heat.
8. Cook the onion and garlic for 2 minutes.
9. Combine the sauce ingredients in a pan over medium heat.
10. Simmer while stirring for 3 minutes.
11. Pour the sauce over the turkey and serve.

Serving Suggestion:

Serve with roasted zucchini slices.

Tip:

Use freshly squeezed lemon juice for this recipe.

Italian Chicken

Don't make the mistake of thinking that this chicken lacks in flavor. It's a lot tastier than it looks!

Prep Time and Cooking Time: 1 hour and 20 minutes | Serves: 4

Ingredients to Use:

- 4 chicken breast fillets
- 16 oz. Italian salad dressing
- 1 teaspoon dried rosemary

Step-by-Step Directions

1. Coat the chicken with dressing.
2. Sprinkle with rosemary.
3. Cover and refrigerate for 1 hour.
4. Transfer the chicken to the air fryer oven.
5. Select bake function.
6. Cook at 370°F for 7 minutes.
7. Flip and cook for another 7 minutes.

Serving Suggestion:

Garnish with rosemary sprigs.

Tip:

You can also use Italian herbs.

Orange Chili Chicken with Veggies

Combine savory, sour and spicy flavors in this tantalizing dish that won't leave you wanting.
Prep Time and Cooking Time: 20 minutes | Serves: 2

Ingredients to Use:

- 2 chicken breast fillets
- 1 clove garlic, minced
- 1 tablespoon ginger, minced
- 1 orange, sliced
- 1 cup bok choy, sliced
- 1/2 cup snap peas, trimmed
- 2 tablespoons tamari sauce
- 2 tablespoons chili garlic sauce

Step-by-Step Directions

1. Add the chicken breast fillets to a foil sheet.
2. Top the chicken with garlic, ginger, and orange slices.
3. Place the bok choy and peas beside the chicken.
4. Mix the tamari and chili garlic sauce.
5. Pour the sauce over the chicken.
6. Wrap the foil around the chicken and vegetables.
7. Place the foil packet inside the air fryer oven.
8. Cook at 370°F for 15 minutes.

Serving Suggestion:

Serve with Jasmine rice.

Tip:

Extend cooking time if chicken is not fully done.

Lemon Turkey with Oregano

This turkey recipe has just the right balance of lemon and herbs that you'd be delighted with.
Prep Time and Cooking Time: 10 minutes | Serves: 4

Ingredients to Use:

- 1 lb. turkey thigh fillet, diced
- 2 teaspoon olive oil
- 1 teaspoon ground oregano
- 1 tablespoon lemon juice

Step-by-Step Directions

1. Toss the turkey cubes in oil.
2. Season with oregano.
3. Drizzle with lemon juice.
4. Transfer to the air fryer oven.
5. Set the air fryer oven to bake.
6. Cook at 350°F for 5 minutes per side.

Serving Suggestion:

Serve with vegetables and rice.

Tip:

Slice chicken into 1-inch pieces.

Chicken with Zucchini & Tomatoes

Healthy and delicious—this can be your go-to recipe when you want to enjoy delicious flavors without any guilt.

Prep Time and Cooking Time: 30 minutes | Serves: 2

Ingredients to Use:

- 1 lb. chicken thigh fillets, diced
- 1 teaspoon dried oregano
- 1 teaspoon lemon juice
- 1/2 cup cherry tomatoes
- 1 zucchini, sliced
- 2 tablespoons olive oil
- Salt and pepper to taste

Step-by-Step Directions

1. Add the chicken to a bowl.
2. Stir in the oregano and lemon juice.
3. Place the chicken in the air fryer oven.
4. Set it to bake.
5. Cook at 370°F for 12 minutes per side.
6. Transfer chicken to a plate.
7. Drizzle the tomatoes and zucchini with oil.
8. Season with salt and pepper.
9. Add to the air fryer basket.
10. Set the oven to air fry.
11. Cook at 320°F for 5 minutes.

Serving Suggestion:

Sprinkle with Italian herbs before serving.

Tip:

You can also use chicken breast fillet for this recipe.

Chicken Fingers

Enjoy crispy chicken fingers without having to use loads of oil.

Prep Time and Cooking Time: 20 minutes | Serves: 6

Ingredients to Use:

- 1 lb. chicken strips
- 1 cup buttermilk
- 1-1/2 cups all-purpose flour
- Garlic salt to taste
- Cooking spray

Step-by-Step Directions

1. Dip chicken strips in buttermilk.
2. Mix the all-purpose flour and garlic salt.
3. Coat the chicken strips in flour mixture.
4. Spray with oil.
5. Add to the air fryer oven.
6. Select air fry function.
7. Cook at 370°F for 7 minutes per side.

Serving Suggestion:

Serve with green salad.

Tip:

You can choose to soak the chicken in buttermilk for 20 minutes before seasoning and cooking.

Mexican Chicken

Take your taste buds on a trip to Mexico with this amazing recipe.

Prep Time and Cooking Time: 20 minutes | Serves: 2

Ingredients to Use:

- 2 chicken breast fillets
- 1 teaspoon chili powder
- Salt and pepper to taste
- 1 cup salsa
- 1 cup black beans, rinsed and drained
- 1 cup corn kernels
- 1/2 cup Mexican cheese, shredded

Step-by-Step Directions

1. Add the chicken on top of a foil sheet.
2. Sprinkle with chili powder, salt and pepper.
3. Top with the salsa, black beans and corn.
4. Fold the foil to make a packet.
5. Place this inside the air fryer oven.
6. Select air fry setting.
7. Cook at 370°F for 7 minutes.
8. Flip and foil packet and cook for another

7 minutes.
9. Unwrap the foil.
10. Sprinkle with cheese.
11. Fold the foil and air fry for another 2 minutes.

Serving Suggestion:

Serve with rice.

Tip:

Add more chili powder if you want your Mexican chicken spicier.

Mediterranean Chicken

Spice things up at home with this fantastic Mediterranean chicken that only takes a few minutes to prepare.
Prep Time and Cooking Time: 20 minutes | Serves: 6

Ingredients to Use:

- 2 tablespoons ground cinnamon
- 2 tablespoons ground coriander
- 1 tablespoon ground nutmeg
- 1 tablespoon ground cumin
- Salt and pepper to taste
- chicken breast fillets
- Cooking spray

Step-by-Step Directions

1. Combine the spices, salt and pepper in a bowl.
2. Sprinkle both sides of chicken with this mixture.
3. Spray with oil.
4. Add to the air fryer oven.
5. Select air fry setting.
6. Cook at 370°F for 7 minutes per side.

Serving Suggestion:

Serve with marinara dip.

Tip:

Add chili powder if you like your chicken spicy.

Garlic & Ginger Chicken Wings

This well-marinated chicken dish can surely satisfy you and your family.
Prep Time and Cooking Time: 45 minutes | Serves: 6

Ingredients to Use:

- 2 tablespoons flour
- Salt and pepper to taste
- 1 tablespoon baking powder
- 1 lb. chicken wings

Sauce

- 1/2 cup soy sauce
- 2 tablespoons ginger, grated
- 1/2 cup brown sugar
- 3 cloves garlic, minced
- 2 tablespoons hot pepper sauce

Step-by-Step Directions

1. Mix flour, salt, pepper and baking powder in a bowl.
2. Coat wings with this mixture.
3. Place the wings in the air fryer oven.
4. Select air fry function.
5. Cook at 380°F for 25 minutes, and flip once or twice.
6. While waiting, mix the sauce ingredients in a bowl.
7. Toss the chicken wings in the sauce.
8. Put these back to the oven.
9. Select bake setting.
10. Cook at 350°F for 5 minutes.

Serving Suggestion:

Garnish with chopped scallions.

Tip:

You can also use honey in place of brown sugar.

Chapter 7: Fish & Seafood Dishes

Baked Swordfish Fillet with Cream Sauce

You won't run out wonderful things to say about this dish—swordfish baked with lemon slices and cream sauce.

Prep Time and Cooking Time: 20 minutes | Serves: 4

Ingredients to Use:

- 4 swordfish fillets
- Salt and pepper to taste
- 4 tablespoons butter
- 1/4 cup heavy cream
- 2 cloves garlic, minced
- 1 tablespoon mustard
- 1-1/2 tablespoons lemon juice

Step-by-Step Directions

1. Select bake setting in your air fryer oven.
2. Preheat it to 400 degrees F.
3. Place the fish fillets in a baking dish.
4. Season with salt and pepper.
5. In a pan over medium heat, melt the butter.
6. Stir in the rest of the ingredients.
7. Simmer for 3 minutes.
8. Pour the sauce over the fish.
9. Place inside the air fryer oven.
10. Bake for 10 minutes.

Serving Suggestion:

Sprinkle chopped parsley on top.

Tip:

If fish is frozen, thaw completely and dry with paper towels before preparing.

Baked Miso Tuna

This dish will fill you up and at the same time, satisfy your cravings.

Prep Time and Cooking Time: 1 hour and 15 minutes | Serves: 4

Ingredients to Use:

- 2 tuna steaks
- 1/2 tablespoon miso paste
- 2 tablespoons mirin
- 1 tablespoon garlic, minced
- 1 teaspoon rice wine
- 1/2 teaspoon vinegar

Step-by-Step Directions

1. Add tuna steaks to a baking pan.
2. Combine remaining ingredients in a bowl.
3. Pour the marinade over the tuna.
4. Cover and refrigerate for 1 hour.
5. Transfer to the air fryer oven.
6. Choose bake setting.
7. Cook at 360 degrees F for 5 to 7 minutes per side.

Serving Suggestion:

Garnish with chopped green onion.

Tip:

Tuna steaks should be at least ½ inch thick.

Tuna Casserole

Here's a good source of protein and healthy fats that you can enjoy.

Prep Time and Cooking Time: 10 minutes | Serves: 2

Ingredients to Use:

Casserole

- 10 oz. canned tuna flakes, drained

- 1/4 cup Mexican cheese blend, shredded
- 1/4 cup onion, chopped
- 1/4 teaspoon onion powder
- 1/4 cup celery, chopped
- 2 tablespoons mayonnaise
- 1/4 cup breadcrumbs
- 1 tablespoon Parmesan cheese
- Salt and pepper to taste

Topping

- 1/4 cup cheddar cheese, grated

Step-by-Step Directions

1. Combine all the casserole ingredients in a baking pan.
2. Top with the grated cheese.
3. Set your air fryer oven to bake.
4. Preheat your air fryer oven to 380 degrees F for 5 minutes.
5. Place the baking pan inside the air fryer oven.
6. Bake for 6 to 10 minutes or until cheese has melted.

Serving Suggestion:

Sprinkle with chopped green onion.

Tip:

You can also add a little cayenne pepper to the casserole if you like.

Pesto Fish Fillets with Walnuts

Flavorful and tender, these pesto fish fillets are bound to make everyone in the dinner table go wow.

Prep Time and Cooking Time: 15 minutes | Serves: 2

Ingredients to Use:

- 2 salmon fillets
- Salt and pepper to taste
- 2 tablespoons pesto sauce
- 1 tablespoon mayonnaise
- 1/4 cup walnuts, chopped

Step-by-Step Directions

1. Season fish with salt and pepper.
2. Mix pesto and mayo.
3. Spread pesto sauce on top of fish.
4. Top with walnuts.
5. Place in the air crisper tray.
6. Choose air fry setting.
7. Place the fish in the air fryer oven.
8. Cook at 380 degrees F for 10 minutes.

Serving Suggestion:

Sprinkle with Parmesan cheese before serving.

Tip:

Dry the fish thoroughly with paper towel before seasoning.

Thai Fish

With minimal preparation, this dish comes out beautifully from your air fryer oven.

Prep Time and Cooking Time: 15 minutes | Serves: 2

Ingredients to Use:

- 1 teaspoon soy sauce
- 2 teaspoons fish sauce
- 1 tablespoon oyster sauce
- 1 clove garlic, minced
- 1/2 tablespoon lime juice
- 1 tablespoon brown sugar
- 2 flounder fillets

Step-by-Step Directions

1. Combine soy sauce, fish sauce, oyster sauce, garlic, lime juice and brown sugar in a bowl.
2. Brush both sides of fish with this mixture.
3. Add the fish fillets to the air fryer oven.
4. Set the air fryer oven to roast.
5. Cook at 370 degrees F for 5 minutes per

side.

Serving Suggestion:

Sprinkle with thinly sliced fresh basil leaves.

Tip:

Use low-sodium fish sauce and soy sauce.

Tuna & Avocado Croquettes

Here's a croquette recipe that won't load you up with carbs.

Prep Time and Cooking Time: 15 minutes | Serves: 4

Ingredients to Use:

- 2 cups canned tuna flakes
- 1/4 teaspoon onion powder
- 1/2 avocado, pitted
- 2 tablespoons lemon juice
- 1/4 cup roasted almonds, chopped
- 1/2 cup breadcrumbs
- Salt and pepper to taste

Step-by-Step Directions

1. Combine all the ingredients in a bowl.
2. Form balls from the mixture.
3. Set your air fryer oven to air fry.
4. Place the tuna balls in the air crisper tray.
5. Cook at 380 degrees F for 8 minutes or until golden.

Serving Suggestion:

Serve with marinara dip.

Tip:

You can also add chopped onion in the mixture.

Cod Fillet with Curry Butter

This delicious cod recipe is ready in under 30 minutes.

Prep Time and Cooking Time: 20 minutes | Serves: 2

Ingredients to Use:

- 1 tablespoon butter, melted
- 1/4 teaspoon curry powder
- 1/8 teaspoon paprika
- Pinch garlic powder
- Salt to taste
- 2 cod fillets

Step-by-Step Directions

1. Combine butter, curry powder, paprika, garlic powder and salt in a bowl.
2. Coat cod fillets with this mixture.
3. Add cod fillets to the air fryer oven.
4. Set it to roast.
5. Cook at 360 degrees F for 4 to 5 minutes per side.
6. Drizzle with cooking liquid and serve.

Serving Suggestion:

Sprinkle with thinly sliced basil.

Tip:

Add more curry powder if you like your fish spicier.

Cod with Soy Ginger Sauce

This Asian style cod recipe will give you outstanding flavors you can't get enough of.

Prep Time and Cooking Time: 15 minutes | Serves: 2

Ingredients to Use:

- 1 tablespoon butter, melted
- 1-1/2 tablespoons rice wine
- 2 teaspoons honey
- 1 tablespoon soy sauce
- 2 cod fillets
- 1 tablespoon ginger, sliced thinly

Step-by-Step Directions

1. Combine butter, rice wine, honey and soy sauce in a bowl.
2. Place the cod fillets on top of a foil sheet.

3. Sprinkle the ginger slices on top.
4. Pour the butter sauce over the fish.
5. Fold the foil to wrap the fish.
6. Pinch sides to seal.
7. Place in the air fryer oven.
8. Select air fry setting.
9. Cook at 360 degrees F for 10 minutes.

Serving Suggestion:

Garnish with cilantro.

Tip:

You can also add sliced onions inside the packet.

Lemon Caper Fish Fillet

Your whole family will be delighted with this light yet delicious fish dish.

Prep Time and Cooking Time: 10 minutes | Serves: 2

Ingredients to Use:

- 2 cod fillets
- Salt and pepper to taste
- 1-1/2 tablespoons butter
- 1/2 teaspoon lemon zest
- 3 tablespoons lemon juice
- 1 tablespoon capers

Step-by-Step Directions

1. Spray fish with oil.
2. Season with salt and pepper.
3. Place the fish inside the air fryer oven.
4. Choose air fry setting.
5. Cook at 360 degrees F for 3 minutes per side.
6. In a pan over medium heat, add the butter.
7. Once melted, stir in lemon zest, lemon juice and capers.
8. Simmer for 1 minute.
9. Transfer fish to a serving plate.
10. Pour sauce over the fish and serve.

Serving Suggestion:

Sprinkle with pepper.

Tip:

Extend cooking time until fish is flaky.

Sweet & Sour Salmon

When you want a change in your weekly menu, here's a dish that will do the trick.

Prep Time and Cooking Time: 20 minutes | Serves: 4

Ingredients to Use:

- 4 salmon fillets, sliced into strips
- Salt and pepper to taste
- 2 tablespoons tapioca starch

Sauce

- 1 teaspoon olive oil
- 2 tablespoons garlic, minced
- 2 tablespoons ginger, grated
- 2 tablespoons sugar
- 2 tablespoons oyster sauce
- 4 tablespoons black vinegar

Step-by-Step Directions

1. Season salmon with salt and pepper.
2. Coat salmon with tapioca starch.
3. Place salmon inside air fryer oven.
4. Choose air fry option.
5. Cook at 400 degrees F for 3 to 4 minutes per side.
6. In a pan over medium heat, add the olive oil.
7. Once hot, cook the garlic and ginger for 1 minute.
8. Stir in sugar, oyster sauce and vinegar.
9. Toss salmon in the sauce and serve.

Serving Suggestion:

Sprinkle with crispy garlic flakes.

Tip:

You can also use all purpose flour in place of tapioca starch.

Chinese-Style Roasted Salmon

Roasted salmon drenched in sweet savory sauce—this will make you feel like you're inside a fancy Chinese restaurant.
Prep Time and Cooking Time: 20 minutes | Serves: 4

Ingredients to Use:

- 4 salmon fillets
- Salt and pepper to taste
- 1 tablespoon vegetable oil
- 2 stalks green onion, chopped
- 3 slices ginger
- 1/4 cup carrot, sliced into strips
- 2 tablespoons soy sauce paste
- 2 tablespoons soy sauce
- 4 tablespoons mirin
- 2 tablespoons rice wine
- 1/4 cup water

Step-by-Step Directions

1. Season both sides of salmon with salt and pepper.
2. Add salmon to the air fryer oven.
3. Select roast setting.
4. Cook at 380 degrees F for 15 minutes, flipping once.
5. Pour oil into a pan over medium heat.
6. Cook ginger, green onion and carrot for 1 minute, stirring often.
7. Stir in the rest of the ingredients.
8. Simmer for 4 minutes.
9. Pour sauce over the salmon and serve.

Serving Suggestion:

Garnish with chopped scallions.

Tip:

Dry salmon with paper towel before seasoning with salt and pepper.

Fish in Lime Butter Sauce

Things don't get easier than this recipe—fish in lime butter sauce.
Prep Time and Cooking Time: 20 minutes | Serves: 4

Ingredients to Use:

- 1 tablespoon butter, melted
- 1 teaspoon paprika
- 1/2 teaspoon garlic powder
- 1/2 teaspoon chili powder
- 1/4 teaspoon cumin
- Salt and pepper to taste
- 4 cod fillets

Sauce

- 1-1/2 tablespoons butter, melted
- 1 tablespoon lime juice
- 1 teaspoon dried parsley flakes

Step-by-Step Directions

1. Combine all the fish ingredients except cod in a bowl.
2. Brush cod with the mixture.
3. Place cod in the air fryer oven.
4. Select grill setting.
5. Cook at 380 degrees F for 3 to 4 minutes per side.
6. Mix the sauce ingredients in a bowl.
7. Microwave on high for 30 seconds.
8. Pour the butter parsley sauce over the fish and serve.

Serving Suggestion:

Garnish with lemon wedges.

Tip:

You can also use other types of white fish fillet for this recipe.

Baked Chinese Fish Fillet

This baked fish fillet will not leave you wanting!
Prep Time and Cooking Time: 20 minutes | Serves: 2

Ingredients to Use:

- 2 swordfish fillets
- 1 tablespoon rice wine
- 2 tablespoon olive oil
- 2 tablespoons ginger, grated
- 1/4 cup dark soy sauce
- 2 tablespoon Shaoxing wine
- 1 tablespoon sugar
- Salt to taste
- 1 tablespoon corn starch mixed with 1/4 cup water

Step-by-Step Directions

1. Brush both sides of fish with rice wine.
2. Add to the air crisper tray.
3. Select bake setting.
4. Cook at 380 degrees F for 5 minutes.
5. Flip and cook for another 5 minutes.
6. Transfer to a serving plate.
7. In a pan over medium heat, sauté ginger and green onion in oil.
8. Stir in the rest of the ingredients.
9. Simmer for 3 minutes.
10. Pour sauce over the fish and serve.

Serving Suggestion:

Garnish with slices green onions.

Tip:

You can also use regular cooking wine if Shaoxing wine is not available.

Fish Nachos

Here's a different way to enjoy fish sticks—serve it nacho style.
Prep Time and Cooking Time: 15 minutes | Serves: 2

Ingredients to Use:

- 8 frozen fish sticks
- 1/4 cup Mexican cheese blend
- 1/4 cup tomato, chopped
- 1/4 cup sour cream
- 1/2 cup avocado, diced
- 2 tablespoons jalapeno, chopped
- 2 tablespoons green onion, chopped
- 2 tablespoons cilantro, chopped

Step-by-Step Directions

1. Add the fish sticks to the air crisper tray.
2. Select air fry setting.
3. Cook at the fish sticks at 380 degrees F for 4 minutes per side or until crispy and golden.
4. Transfer fish to a cutting board.
5. Chop and place on a serving platter.
6. Sprinkle cheese on top.
7. Select bake setting.
8. Bake in the air fryer oven for 1 minute.
9. Spread the sour cream on top.
10. Top with the remaining ingredients and serve.

Serving Suggestion:

Drizzle with hot sauce.

Tip:

You can also use cheddar cheese for this recipe.

Tuna with Ponzu Sauce

This will surely become a regular dish in your weekly menu.
Prep Time and Cooking Time: 20 minutes | Serves: 2

Ingredients to Use:

- 1/2 cup Japanese Ponzu sauce
- 1 tablespoon olive oil
- 1-1/2 tablespoons ginger, grated
- 2 tuna steaks

Step-by-Step Directions

1. Mix Japanese Ponzu sauce, olive oil and ginger in a bowl.
2. Marinate fish in the mixture for 1 hour.
3. Preheat your air fryer to 400 degrees F for 2 minutes.
4. Select air fry setting.

5. Cook fish for 3 minutes per side.

Serving Suggestion:

Sprinkle with chopped green onion and sesame seeds.

Tip:

If Ponzu sauce is not available, you can replace this with a mixture of ¼ cup soy sauce, 3 tablespoons lemon juice and 3 tablespoons mirin.

Cheesy Kimchi Fish

East meets West in this simple but enticing dish that you'd love each time.

Prep Time and Cooking Time: 15 minutes | Serves: 4

Ingredients to Use:

- 4 cod fillets
- Salt and pepper to taste
- 1/2 cup kimchi, chopped
- 1/2 cup mozzarella cheese, shredded

Step-by-Step Directions

1. Arrange the fish in a baking pan.
2. Season with salt and pepper.
3. Top with kimchi.
4. Sprinkle cheese on top.
5. Place the baking pan inside the air fryer oven.
6. Select bake function.
7. Bake at 380 degrees F for 5 minutes.

Serving Suggestion:

Garnish with chopped green onions.

Tip:

Internal temperature of fish should be at least 145 degrees F.

Korean Barbecue Tuna Patties

Tender and flavorful, these Asian tuna patties will surely be a star in the dinner table.

Prep Time and Cooking Time: 20 minutes | Serves: 4

Ingredients to Use:

- 6 oz. canned tuna flakes, drained
- 1 tablespoons Korean barbecue sauce
- 1 egg, beaten
- 1/4 cup green onion, chopped
- Pepper to taste
- 1/2 cup breadcrumbs
- 2 tablespoons mayonnaise
- 1/4 teaspoon garlic powder

Step-by-Step Directions

1. Add all the ingredients to a large bowl.
2. Form patties from the mixture.
3. Select air fry setting.
4. Set temperature to 380 degrees F.
5. Add the tuna patties to the air crisper tray.
6. Cook for 10 minutes, flipping once.

Serving Suggestion:

Serve with spicy mayo dip.

Tip:

You can also add hot sauce to the patty mixture.

Baked Fish with Garlic & Basil

This only takes minimal effort to prepare.

Prep Time and Cooking Time: 30 minutes | Serves: 6

Ingredients to Use:

- 2 lb. white fish fillets
- 1 teaspoon sweet paprika
- 1 teaspoon ground coriander
- 1-1/2 teaspoon dried oregano
- Salt and pepper to taste
- 10 cloves garlic, minced
- 15 basil, chopped
- 1 tablespoon lemon juice
- 6 tablespoons olive oil
- 2 green onions, chopped

- 1 red bell pepper, sliced
- 1 green bell pepper, sliced

Step-by-Step Directions

1. Mix paprika, coriander, oregano, salt and pepper in a bowl.
2. Sprinkle both sides of fish with this mixture.
3. Marinate in the refrigerator for 1 hour.
4. In a bowl, mix garlic, basil, lemon juice and olive oil.
5. Preheat your air fryer oven to 425 degrees F.
6. Select bake function.
7. Arrange the green onions and bell peppers in the baking pan.
8. Top with the fish.
9. Bake in the oven for 15 minutes.
10. Pour garlic basil sauce over the fish and serve.

Serving Suggestion:

Serve with salad or pasta.

Tip:

You can also use fresh basil leaves to garnish the dish.

Korean Yellow Croaker Fish

For sure, you and your family will enjoy these Korean style yellow croaker fish that's ready in a few minutes.
Prep Time and Cooking Time: 20 minutes | Serves: 3

Ingredients to Use:

- 6 yellow croaker fish
- 1-1/2 teaspoons Korean chilli garlic paste
- 1 tablespoon rice wine
- 1/2 teaspoon soy sauce
- 2 tablespoons honey

Step-by-Step Directions

1. Brush fish with rice wine.
2. Let sit for 5 minutes.
3. In a bowl, mix the remaining ingredients.
4. Spread the sauce on both sides of the fish.
5. Place the fish inside the air fryer oven.
6. Select air fry option.
7. Set temperature to 400 degrees F.
8. Cook for 5 minutes per side.

Serving Suggestion:

Serve with lemon and soy sauce mixture for dipping.

Tip:

Make shallow slices on the fish before spreading with the sauce.

Cheesy Tuna & Egg Bake

This dish is so good you probably would want another round!
Prep Time and Cooking Time: 15 minutes | Serves: 2

Ingredients to Use:

- 10 oz. canned tuna flakes
- 1 egg, beaten
- 1/4 cup breadcrumbs
- 1 teaspoon hot sauce
- 3 tablespoons mayonnaise
- 1/4 cup celery, chopped
- 1/4 cup mozzarella cheese

Step-by-Step Directions

1. Combine all the ingredients except the egg in a bowl.
2. Transfer mixture to a baking pan.
3. Crack the egg on top of the mixture.
4. Place inside the air fryer oven.
5. Set the air fryer oven to bake.
6. Cook at 380 degrees F for 10 minutes.

Serving Suggestion:

Garnish with chopped scallions.

Tip:

Make sure egg is fully cooked before serving. Extend cooking time if necessary.

Tuna & Black Bean Bake

This dish is as delicious as it is colorful!

Prep Time and Cooking Time: 30 minutes | Serves: 4

Ingredients to Use:

- 10 oz. canned tuna flakes, drained
- 1/2 cup canned black beans, rinsed and drained
- 1/2 cup sour cream
- 1/2 cup tomatoes, chopped
- Salt and pepper to taste
- 1/2 cup Mexican blend cheese, shredded

Step-by-Step Directions

1. Combine all the ingredients in a baking pan.
2. Place inside the air fryer oven.
3. Select bake function.
4. Set the temperature to 360 degrees F.
5. Cook for 15 minutes.

Serving Suggestion:

Serve with tortilla chips.

Tip:

You can also use salmon flakes for this recipe.

Tuna & Corn Croquettes

If there's a party at your home, you can prepare these tuna and corn croquettes.

Prep Time and Cooking Time: 15 minutes | Serves: 4

Ingredients to Use:

- 10 oz. canned tuna flakes
- 1/4 cup breadcrumbs
- 1/4 cup corn kernels
- 1 egg, beaten
- 1/4 teaspoon dried basil
- 1/4 teaspoon garlic powder
- 2 tablespoons mayonnaise

Step-by-Step Directions

1. Mix all the ingredients in a bowl.
2. Form balls from the mixture.
3. Place the balls in the air crisper tray.
4. Set the air fryer oven to air fry.
5. Cook at 360 degrees F for 10 minutes, turning once.

Serving Suggestion:

Serve with sriracha mayo dip.

Tip:

You can also add red pepper flakes to the mixture.

Egg & Tuna Salad

This is a low-carb version of your favorite egg and tuna salad.

Prep Time and Cooking Time: 10 minutes | Serves: 2

Ingredients to Use:

- 2 cans tuna flakes, drained
- 2 tablespoons pickled jalapenos, chopped
- 1/4 cup tomato, chopped
- 1 hard-boiled egg, chopped
- 1 tablespoon mayonnaise
- Salt and pepper to taste
- 1/4 cup cheddar, grated
- 1/4 cup mozzarella cheese

Step-by-Step Directions

1. Add all the ingredients to a bowl.
2. Mix well.
3. Choose air fry setting.
4. Preheat your air fryer to 400 degrees F for 2 minutes.
5. Transfer mixture to a ramekin.
6. Place inside the air fryer oven.
7. Cook for 4 minutes.

Serving Suggestion:

Garnish with chopped parsley.

Tip:

You can also sprinkle with Parmesan cheese.

Cheesy Fish Salsa

This fish recipe combines two things that you love cheese and salsa!

Prep Time and Cooking Time: 15 minutes | Serves: 2

Ingredients to Use:

- 2 cod fillets
- 1 cup salsa
- 1/4 cup Mexican cheese blend

Step-by-Step Directions

1. Arrange the cod fillets in a baking pan.
2. Top with the salsa.
3. Sprinkle cheese on top of salsa.
4. Select air fry setting in your air fryer oven.
5. Cook at 360 degrees F for 10 minutes.

Serving Suggestion:

Garnish with fresh basil leaves.

Tip:

You can also use haddock fillet for this recipe.

Fish with Cordia Dichotoma

This is a Taiwanese fish dish that you'd enjoy with every spoonful.

Prep Time and Cooking Time: 15 minutes | Serves: 2

Ingredients to Use:

- 2 cod fillets
- 2 teaspoon rice wine
- 2 tablespoons Taiwanese pickled Cordia Dichotoma
- 2 tablespoon pickled seed juice
- 2 teaspoon ginger, thinly sliced

Step-by-Step Directions

1. Add the cod fillets on top of a foil sheet.
2. Pour rice wine, Cordia Dichotoma and pickled seed juice on top of the fish.
3. Sprinkle the ginger slices on top.
4. Wrap the foil and pinch the sides to seal.
5. Place the foil packet inside the air fryer oven.
6. Select bake setting.
7. Set it to 360 degrees F.
8. Cook for 8 to 10 minutes.

Serving Suggestion:

Sprinkle sliced green onion on top.

Tip:

Let cool for 10 minutes before unwrapping.

Chili Garlic Sardines

This dish is a good source of omega 3 fatty acids and protein.

Prep Time and Cooking Time: 15 minutes | Serves: 2

Ingredients to Use:

- 2 cans sardines in oil
- 1 tablespoon sesame oil
- 2 cloves garlic, minced
- ¼ cup green onion, chopped
- 1 tablespoon Gochujang Korean chili paste
- 1 teaspoon soy sauce
- 2 tablespoons honey
- 3 tablespoons water

Step-by-Step Directions

1. Add the sardines in a greased pizza pan.
2. Place inside the air fryer oven.
3. Select air fry setting.
4. Cook at 400 degrees F for 4 to 5 minutes per side.

5. Pour the oil into a pan over medium heat.
6. Cook the garlic and green onion for 1 minute, stirring often.
7. Stir in the rest of the ingredients.
8. Turn off heat.
9. Pour the sauce over the fish and serve.

Serving Suggestion:

Garnish with sliced green onions.

Tip:

Arrange the sardines in a single layer to cook evenly.

Fish with Butter & Cayenne Pepper Sauce

This is a spectacular dish that only takes a few minutes to prepare.
Prep Time and Cooking Time: 15 minutes | Serves: 2

Ingredients to Use:

- 2 Swai fish fillets
- Salt and pepper to taste
- 2 tablespoons butter, melted
- 2 tablespoon rice wine
- 2 tablespoon lemon juice
- 1/4 teaspoon cayenne pepper

Step-by-Step Directions

1. Place the fish fillets in a baking pan.
2. Season with salt and pepper.
3. Combine the butter, rice wine, lemon juice and cayenne pepper in a bowl.
4. Pour the sauce over the fish.
5. Place inside the air fryer oven.
6. Choose bake setting.
7. Bake at 380 degrees F for 6 to 8 minutes.

Serving Suggestion:

Sprinkle with chopped parsley.

Tip:

Use white wine if rice wine is not available.

Garlic Shrimp Scampi

This garlic shrimp scampi is an incredible seafood dish that's bursting with so much flavor.
Prep Time and Cooking Time: 15 minutes | Serves: 4

Ingredients to Use:

- 4 tablespoons butter, melted
- 1 teaspoon red pepper flakes
- 3 tablespoons garlic, minced
- 1/2 lb. shrimp, peeled and deveined
- 1/4 cup chicken broth
- 3 tablespoons capers
- 3 tablespoons lemon juice

Step-by-Step Directions

1. Mix the butter, red pepper flakes and garlic in a cake pan.
2. Place inside the air fryer oven.
3. Select air fry setting.
4. Cook at 400 degrees F for 2 minutes.
5. Stir in the shrimp and remaining ingredients.
6. Choose bake function.
7. Bake at 370 degrees F for 6 to 8 minutes.

Serving Suggestion:

Garnish with fresh basil.

Tip:

Use low-sodium chicken broth.

Garlic Miso Tuna

Combine miso and garlic for the ultimate tuna dish that you'll never get bored with.
Prep Time and Cooking Time: 15 minutes | Serves: 3

Ingredients to Use:

- 1 clove garlic, minced
- 1/2 teaspoon miso
- 1-1/2 tablespoons mayo

- Pepper to taste
- 3 tuna steaks

Step-by-Step Directions

1. Mix the garlic, miso, mayo and pepper in a bowl.
2. Spread mixture on top of tuna steak.
3. Place on top of the air crisper tray.
4. Turn to air fry setting.
5. Cook at 380 degrees F for 6 to 8 minutes.

Serving Suggestion:

Sprinkle fried garlic flakes and chopped green onions on top.

Tip:

You can also use salmon fillets for this recipe.

Korean Fried Shrimp

Now you can enjoy Korean fried shrimp without any guilt!
Prep Time and Cooking Time: 20 minutes | Serves: 4

Ingredients to Use:

- 16 shrimp, peeled and deveined
- 1 egg, beaten
- 1/4 cup tapioca starch

Sauce

- 1 tablespoon sesame oil
- 1/4 cup onion, chopped
- 3 cloves garlic, minced
- 2 teaspoons Gochujang Korean hot pepper paste
- 2 tablespoons honey
- 2 tablespoons oyster sauce
- 2 tablespoons soy sauce
- 1 tablespoons lemon juice
- 2 tablespoons water

Step-by-Step Directions

1. Dip shrimp in egg.
2. Coat with tapioca starch.
3. Add to the air crisper tray.
4. Select air fry setting.
5. Cook at 400 degrees F for 4 to 5 minutes per side.
6. To make the sauce, add oil to a pan over medium heat.
7. Cook onion and garlic for 1 minute, stirring often.
8. Stir in the rest of the ingredients.
9. Simmer for 3 minutes.
10. Toss the shrimp in the sauce and serve.

Serving Suggestion:

Garnish with green onion and sesame seeds.

Tip:

Extend cooking time if using frozen shrimp.

Crispy Cod Fillets

Crunch with every bite—this is what you'll get from this amazing but easy to prepare dish.
Prep Time and Cooking Time: 15 minutes | Serves: 2

Ingredients to Use:

- 2 cod fillets
- 1 teaspoon Sriracha hot sauce
- 1 tablespoon mayo
- 1/2 teaspoon garlic powder
- Salt to taste
- 1/4 cup breadcrumbs

Step-by-Step Directions

1. Combine the hot sauce, mayo, garlic powder and salt in a bowl.
2. Sprinkle cod fillets with this mixture.
3. Dredge with breadcrumbs
4. Add breaded cod fillets in the air fryer oven.
5. Choose air fry setting.
6. Cook at 380 degrees F for 10 minutes.

Serving Suggestion:

Serve with spicy mayo dip.

Tip:

You can also make this ahead of time by freezing bread fish and air frying when ready to serve.

Cracker Crusted Fish Fillet

It's not often that you get this incredible idea to use crackers for breading for your fish!
Prep Time and Cooking Time: X minutes | Serves: X

Ingredients to Use:

- 4 cod fillets
- 2 tablespoons rice wine
- Salt and pepper to taste
- 3 tablespoons garlic, minced
- 1/4 cup saltine crackers, crushed
- 3 tablespoons butter, melted

Step-by-Step Directions

1. Drizzle cod with rice wine.
2. Season with salt and pepper.
3. In a bowl, mix the garlic, crackers and butter.
4. Press mixture on top of side of fish.
5. Choose air fry setting in your air fryer oven.
6. Add fish to the air crisper tray.
7. Cook at 280 degrees f for 15 minutes.

Serving Suggestion:

Garnish with parsley flakes.

Tip:

You can also use other white fish fillets for this recipe.

Chapter 8: Meatless Dishes

Vegan Mini Lasagna

This recipe offers a heartily healthier version to an all-time comfort food.

Prep Time and Cooking Time: 30 minutes | Serves: 1

Ingredients to Use:

- 2 lasagna noodles, halved and cooked
- 1/2 cup pasta sauce
- 1 cup baby spinach leaves, chopped
- 3 tablespoons zucchini
- 1 cup fresh basil leaves, chopped
- 1/4 cup tofu ricotta

Step-by-Step Directions

1. Spread pasta sauce on a mini loaf pan.
2. Alternately layer the noodles with a mix of pasta sauce, spinach, zucchini, basil, and tofu ricotta.
3. Cover the loaf pan with aluminium foil.
4. Set the oven at 400°F on bake mode for 3 to 5 minutes.

Serving Suggestion:

Garnish with chopped parsley.

Tip:

Use egg-free lasagna noodles.

Baked Zesty Tofu

This recipe has all the flavors of the deep-fried version but with none of the oil.

Prep Time and Cooking Time: 40 minutes | Serves: 4

Ingredients to Use:

Sauce

- 2 tablespoons organic sugar
- 1/3 cup lemon juice
- 2 teaspoons arrowroot powder
- 1/2 cup water
- 1 teaspoon lemon zest

Tofu

- 1 tablespoon tamari
- 1 lb. extra-firm tofu, drained and pressed
- 1 tablespoon arrowroot powder

Step-by-Step Directions

1. Combine all the sauce ingredients in a small bowl.
2. Coat the tofu with tamari, and then with arrowroot powder.
3. Set oven in bake function at 390°F.
4. Bake for 10 minutes, shaking halfway through.
5. Heat the tofu and sauce in a skillet over medium to high setting until the sauce thickens.

Serving Suggestion:

Serve with steamed rice and vegetables.

Tip:

Use Meyer lemons to use less sugar.

Potato & Kale Nuggets

This recipe will be a hit to kids and those who are still kids at heart.

Prep Time and Cooking Time: 20 minutes | Serves: 4

Ingredients to Use:

- 1 teaspoon extra virgin olive oil
- 4 cups kale, chopped
- 1 clove garlic, minced
- 1/8 cup almond milk
- 2 cups potatoes, cooked

- Salt and pepper to taste

Step-by-Step Directions

1. Sauté the garlic and kale in oil for 2 or 3 minutes.
2. Mash the potato, adding milk, salt and pepper.
3. Combine the two mixtures, and then roll into 1-inch nuggets.
4. Cook on bake mode at 390°F for 12 to 15 minutes.

Serving Suggestion:

Serve with steamed rice or quinoa.

Tip:

You may omit the olive oil, if desired.

Crunchy Sushi Rolls

These veggie rolls are fun to make and filling to eat.
Prep Time and Cooking Time: 1 hour, 10 minutes | Serves: 3

Ingredients to Use:

Kale Salad

- 3/4 teaspoon toasted sesame seeds
- 1/4 teaspoon ground ginger
- 1/2 teaspoon rice vinegar
- 1/8 teaspoon garlic powder
- 3/4 teaspoon soy sauce
- 1-1/2 cups kale, ribbed and chopped

Sushi Rolls

- 3 sheets sushi nori
- Sushi rice, cooked
- 1/2 Haas avocado, sliced
- 1/4 cup mayo
- 1/2 cup Panko breadcrumbs

Step-by-Step Directions

1. Massage the kale with the kale salad ingredients until wilted.
2. Spread a layer of thin rice on the nori sheet, leaving a half-inch of naked seaweed along one edge.
3. Layer the kale salad, and then top with avocado slices.
4. Roll up the sushi.
5. Coat with mayo, and then with Panko.
6. Cook on air fryer, setting at 390°F for 10 minutes.
7. Let it cool before slicing.

Serving Suggestion:

Serve with soy sauce dipping.

Tip:

Add sriracha sauce to the mayo to taste.

Crispy BBQ Soy Curls

This dish is so versatile that you can pair it with almost anything.
Prep Time and Cooking Time: 21 minutes| Serves: 2

Ingredients to Use:

- 1 cup soy curls
- 1 cup warm water
- 1 teaspoon vegetable broth
- 1/4 cup vegan barbecue sauce

Step-by-Step Directions

1. Soak soy curls in warm water with vegetable broth for 10 minutes.
2. Drain and shred into a mixing bowl.
3. Cook on air fry setting at 400°F for 3 minutes.
4. Put back in mixing bowl and coat with barbecue sauce.
5. Air fry for another 5 minutes.

Serving Suggestion:

Serve with potato salad and collard greens.

Tip:

You can use plain water instead of broth.

Vegan Omelettes

This recipe makes it easy to give up egg and cheese.
Prep Time and Cooking Time: 31 minutes | Serves: 3

Ingredients to Use:

- 1/2 block of organic tofu
- 1/2 cup spinach, finely chopped
- 3 tablespoons nutritional yeast
- 1/2 teaspoon cumin
- 1/4 cup chickpea flour
- 1/2 teaspoon turmeric
- 1/4 teaspoon onion powder
- 1/4 teaspoon basil
- 1/4 teaspoon garlic powder
- 1 tablespoon apple cider vinegar
- 1/2 cup vegan cheese, grated
- 1 tablespoon water
- Salt and pepper to taste

Step-by-Step Directions

1. Blend all the ingredients in a processor, except for the spinach and cheese.
2. Combine the batter with spinach and cheese.
3. Make six omelettes into desired shape.
4. Cook on bake mode set at 370°F for 4 minutes on each side.

Serving Suggestion:

Serve in a sandwich.

Tip:

Use a cookie cutter to shape your omelettes.

Lentil Meatballs with BBQ Sauce

This tastes just like the savory meatballs you grew up eating.
Prep Time and Cooking Time: 45 minutes | Serves: 5

Ingredients to Use:

- 1 cup white onion, diced and sautéed
- 1 clove garlic, minced and sautéed
- 1 tablespoon tomato paste
- 1/2 cup dried mushrooms, chopped and boiled
- 1 cup dry brown lentils, boiled
- 2 cups vegetable broth
- 1/2 cup vital wheat gluten
- 2 tablespoons avocado oil
- 3 tablespoons vegan BBQ sauce
- 1 tablespoon vegan low-sodium soy sauce
- 1 teaspoon dried parsley
- 1 teaspoon onion powder
- 1/2 teaspoon smoked paprika
- Salt and pepper to taste

Step-by-Step Directions

1. Blend all the ingredients in a food processor until chunky.
2. Make meat balls, each using 2 tablespoons of the mixture.
3. Select grill function on your air fryer oven.
4. Cook at 350°F for 12 minutes.

Serving Suggestion:

Slather with vegan barbecue sauce.

Tip:

You can use vegan Worcestershire sauce, if available.

Cajun Fishless Filets with Pecan Crust

This quick and easy recipe is a mix of tasty, flaky, and crispy texture.
Prep Time and Cooking Time: 20 minutes | Serves: 3

Ingredients to Use:

- 3/4 cup water
- 1 teaspoon Cajun seasoning blend

- 3/4 cup pecans, minced
- 3 tablespoons flax seed, ground
- 1/4 cup plus 2 tablespoons cornmeal, finely ground
- 10.1 oz. Gardein Golden Fishless Filets

Step-by-Step Directions

1. Make batter by combining all the ingredients except for the filets.
2. Coat the filets with the batter.
3. Cook on roast mode at 390°F for 10 minutes.
4. Flip and roast for another 3 to 5 minutes.

Serving Suggestion:

Serve with rice and hot sauce.

Tip:

You can check if the center is piping hot—meaning it's cooked—by poking with a fork.

Curried Cauliflower

Enjoy the classic Indian flavor with this one pan recipe.
Prep Time and Cooking Time: 20 minutes | Serves: 3

Ingredients to Use:

- 12 oz. cauliflower florets
- 1 cup vegetable stock
- 1 cup sweet corn kernels
- 3/4 cup light coconut milk
- 1 teaspoon garlic purée
- 3 scallions, sliced
- 1-1/2 teaspoon garam masala
- 1 teaspoon turmeric
- 1 teaspoon mild curry powder
- Salt to taste

Step-by-Step Directions

1. Combine all the ingredients a large bowl until vegetables are fully coated.
2. Put in a deep dish.
3. Select the air fry function, and set the temperature to 375°F.
4. Cook the vegetables for 12 to 15 minutes.

Serving Suggestion:

Top with dried cranberries and lime wedges.

Tip:

Stir every 3 or so minutes while cooking.

Baked Mushroom Pulled Pork

This recipe gives a similar texture and taste of the real stuff.
Prep Time and Cooking Time: 25 minutes | Serves: 3

Ingredients to Use:

- 2 cloves garlic, minced
- 1/4 teaspoon cayenne pepper
- 2 tablespoons extra virgin olive oil
- 1 teaspoon smoked paprika
- Salt to taste
- 4 king oyster mushrooms, shredded
- 1/4 cup barbecue sauce

Step-by-Step Directions

1. Mix all the ingredients, except barbecue sauce, until mushrooms are coated evenly.
2. Set on a lined baking sheet.
3. Cook on bake mode at 400°F for 10 minutes.
4. Transfer in large pan and sauté with barbecue sauce for 3 to 5 minutes.

Serving Suggestion:

Pair with corn or potatoes and serve with barbecue sauce.

Tip:

You can also serve in a sandwich or with salad.

Vegan Burrito Bowl

Preparing a full meal in a bowl has never been this easy.
Prep Time and Cooking Time: 25 minutes | Serves: 4

Ingredients to Use:

- 8 oz. mushroom, sliced
- 1 cup sweet corn
- 2 cups black beans
- 1 teaspoon onion powder
- 1 cup white onion, chopped
- 1/2 cup red onion, chopped
- 1/2 cup green onion, chopped
- 1 cup tomatoes, diced
- 1/2 teaspoon paprika
- 1 teaspoon chili powder
- 2 teaspoons cumin, ground
- 1 teaspoon garlic, minced
- Salt and pepper to taste

Step-by-Step Directions

1. Combine all the ingredients in a large bowl.
2. Place mixture in air fryer basket.
3. Spritz with avocado oil.
4. Set to air fry function at 370°F.
5. Cook for 15 minutes.

Serving Suggestion:

Serve with quinoa and top with guacamole.

Tip:

Shake the basket halfway through cooking.

Asparagus & Mushroom Stir-Fry

Dinner will be ready in less than 15 minutes with this recipe.
Prep Time and Cooking Time: 12 minutes | Serves: 2

Ingredients to Use:

- 4 stalks asparagus, cut in half
- 50 grams extra firm tofu, cut into strips
- 3 brown mushrooms, sliced
- 4 brussels sprouts, halved
- 2 cloves garlic, minced
- 1/2 teaspoon sesame oil
- 1 teaspoon Italian seasoning
- 1/4 teaspoon soy sauce
- Salt and pepper to taste

Step-by-Step Directions

1. Toss all the ingredients in a bowl to combine.
2. Place in the air fryer basket.
3. Select the air fry option on your oven, and set to 350°F.
4. Cook for 7 or 8 minutes.

Serving Suggestion:

Garnish with toasted sesame seeds.

Tip:

You may extend cooking time depending on your doneness preference.

Tofu & Broccoli Stir-Fry

This is a low-calorie and keto-friendly recipe.
Prep Time and Cooking Time: 30 minutes | Serves: 4

Ingredients to Use:

- 2 heads broccoli
- 1 cup red bell pepper, thinly sliced
- 2 cloves garlic, minced
- 1 onion, diced
- 1 tablespoon rice vinegar
- 2 tablespoon soy sauce
- 1/2 teaspoon ginger, ground
- 1 tablespoon sesame oil
- 12 oz. extra firm tofu

Step-by-Step Directions

1. Toss and coat the vegetables with spices, vinegar, soy sauce.
2. Spritz sesame oil on the air fryer basket.
3. Air fry the tofu at 400°F for 5 minutes each side.

4. Add the vegetables, and then cook at 370°F for 15 to 30 minutes.

Serving Suggestion:

Garnish with roasted sesame seeds.

Tip:

You may extend the cooking time until the vegetables are cooked to desired texture.

Crispy Southern Tofu with BBQ Sauce

This light recipe is reminiscent of a certain Louisville flavor.
Prep Time and Cooking Time: 2 hour, 20 minutes | Serves: 2

Ingredients to Use:

- 1 block extra firm tofu, drained
- 1 tablespoon gluten free tamari
- 1 cup vegetable broth
- 1-1/4 cups corn flakes
- 1 teaspoon onion powder
- 1/4 teaspoon smoked paprika
- 1 tablespoon nutritional yeast
- 1/2 teaspoon celery salt
- 1/4 teaspoon kala namak

Step-by-Step Directions

1. Marinate the tofu in tamari and broth mix for two hours.
2. Blend corn flakes using food processor to make fine powdery crumbs.
3. Combine crumbs with the rest of the ingredients, except for the tofu.
4. Coat tofu by pressing onto the crumb mix.
5. Arrange on a lined baking sheet, and then set oven to bake function.
6. Cook at 350°F for 7 minutes on each side.

Serving Suggestion:

Coat with barbecue sauce.

Tip:

Marinate the tofu overnight.

Mashed Eggplant

This easy recipe is originated in India and is called baingan bharta.
Prep Time and Cooking Time: 45 minutes | Serves: 4

Ingredients to Use:

- 4 medium eggplants, sliced
- 1 tablespoon olive oil
- 1/2 cup peas
- 1/2 cup onion, chopped
- 2 teaspoon lemon juice
- 1 teaspoon serrano peppers
- 1/2 tablespoon coriander powder
- 6 cloves garlic
- 1 teaspoon powder
- Salt to taste

Step-by-Step Directions

1. Cook the eggplants on roast mode at 390°F for 20 to 25 minutes.
2. Mash the eggplant pulps, and then heat on a skillet with oil.
3. Add the rest of the ingredients, and then cook for 2 or 3 minutes.

Serving Suggestion:

Garnish with cilantro leaves and serve hot with naan, roti, or poori.

Tip:

This will last up to 3 days in the refrigerator, and one month in the freezer.

Low-Fat Chinese Noodles

A serving of this filling recipe has 166 calories and only 4 grams of fat.
Prep Time and Cooking Time: 25 minutes | Serves: 6

Ingredients to Use:

- 13 oz. Chinese noodles, precooked
- 5 oz. button mushrooms, washed
- 1 onion, finely chopped
- 5 oz. soya beans, washed and soaked overnight
- 8 oz. carrots, peeled and cut into strips
- 4 tablespoons soy sauce
- 1 tablespoon vegetable stock powder
- 4 tablespoons water

Step-by-Step Directions

1. Dilute the stock powder in water.
2. Place the noodles on the line baking pan.
3. Add the rest of the ingredients.
4. Air fry at 350°F for 15 minutes.

Serving Suggestion:

Drizzle with sriracha.

Tip:

Soak the beans overnight.

Dry Curry with Eggplant

This flavorful recipe is based on a cooking style in South India.
Prep Time and Cooking Time: 17 minutes | Serves: 4

Ingredients to Use:

- 2 cups eggplants, cubed
- 1 large onion, chopped
- 1-1/2 teaspoon cayenne powder
- 1/2 teaspoon cumin seeds
- 2 tablespoons curry powder
- 1/2 teaspoon mustard seeds
- 1/2 teaspoon turmeric powder
- 6 cloves garlic, minced
- 2 tablespoons olive oil
- Salt to taste

Step-by-Step Directions

1. Place the eggplants and onion in a greased air fryer basket.
2. Season with the rest of the ingredients, except for the curry powder and cayenne powder.
3. Cook on air fryer, setting at 390°F for 10 minutes.
4. Mix in the curry powder and cayenne powder.
5. Cook for another 3 minutes.

Serving Suggestion:

Garnish with chopped coriander.

Tip:

Refrigerate for up to 5 days.

Beet Noodles with Balsamic Vinegar

This vibrant recipe enhances the distinct flavor of beets.
Prep Time and Cooking Time: 35 minutes | Serves: 4

Ingredients to Use:

- 2 large beets, peeled and spiralized
- 2 tablespoons balsamic vinegar
- 2 tablespoons olive oil
- Salt and pepper to taste

Step-by-Step Directions

1. Season the beet noodles with vinegar, oil, salt, and pepper.
2. Place the beet on a baking sheet.
3. Cook on roast mode at 350°F for 20 minutes.

Serving Suggestion:

Sprinkle with orange zest and parsley.

Tip:

Use a 5-mm spiralizer blade to make the noodles.

Air Fried Instant Ramen

These crispy and crunchy noodles will compliment any juicy vegetable dish.

Prep Time and Cooking Time: 45 minutes | Serves: 4

Ingredients to Use:

- 4 cups water, boiling
- 4 packs ramen noodles
- 1 tablespoon olive oil

Step-by-Step Directions

1. Put the noodles in boiling water for 5 minutes.
2. Drain, and then toss in oil.
3. Place noodles on aluminium foil, and then put in the air fryer basket.
4. Select air fry function and set temperature to 350°F.
5. Cook for 15 to 20 minutes.

Serving Suggestion:

Serve with meatless chop suey.

Tip:

Cook in batches.

Chickpea Patties

This is a vegan take on the classic burger that can pair easily with any dish.
Prep Time and Cooking Time: 25 minutes | Serves: 3

Ingredients to Use:

- 1 medium sweet potato, boiled and mashed
- 1 cup chickpeas, boiled and mashed
- 1 onion, chopped
- 1 green chili, chopped
- 3 twigs coriander leaves, chopped
- 2 tablespoons chickpea flour
- 1 teaspoon cumin
- Salt to taste

Step-by-Step Directions

1. Combine all the ingredients to make the batter.
2. Make small balls and flatten by pressing in between your palms.
3. Place the patties on a greased air fryer basket.
4. Air fry at 390°F for 8 or 9 minutes.
5. Flip and cook for another 5 or 6 minutes.

Serving Suggestion:

Serve with rice and your favorite sauce for dipping.

Tip:

Soak the chickpeas overnight.

Grilled Veggie Skewers

This recipe spells summertime all year round.
Prep Time and Cooking Time: 35 minutes | Serves: 4

Ingredients to Use:

- 1 medium red onion, cut into 2-inch chunks
- 1 medium yellow squash, cut into 1-inch slices
- 1 medium zucchini, cut into 1-inch slices
- 3 red, yellow, or orange bell peppers, cut into 1-inch slices
- 1/4 cup extra-virgin olive oil
- 2 garlic cloves, pressed
- Salt and pepper to taste

Step-by-Step Directions

1. Season the vegetables and onion with garlic, salt, pepper, and oil.
2. Alternate the onions and vegetables on the skewers.
3. Grill on medium to high heat for 15 minutes, or until slightly charred.

Serving Suggestion:

Serve hot with rice and a dipping sauce.

Tip:

Soak wooden skewers in water for 10

minutes to prevent them from burning.

Grilled Lime Cabbage

This grilled recipe is sure to be a hit, even mong meat lovers.

Prep Time and Cooking Time: 20 minutes | Serves: 4

Ingredients to Use:

- 4 tablespoons olive oil
- 2 tablespoons fresh lime juice
- 1 large Napa cabbage
- 1 tablespoon nam pla fish sauce
- 1 teaspoon fresh ginger, minced or grated
- 2 tablespoons fresh cilantro, stems removed
- teaspoon lemongrass, minced
- Salt to taste

Step-by-Step Directions

1. Make the dressing by whisking together oil, lime juice, fish sauce, ginger, lemongrass, and cilantro.
2. Season the cabbage with oil and salt.
3. Select the grill function at medium to high setting.
4. Grill for 3 to 5 minutes on both sides.
5. Drizzle the dressing or serve on the side.

Serving Suggestion:

Garnish with parsley sprigs.

Tip:

For a vegan option, use soy sauce or liquid aminos instead of fish sauce.

Grilled Purple Caponata

This recipe is a Sicilian specialty that will surely add color and flavor to your table spread.

Prep Time and Cooking Time: 45 minutes | Serves: 8

Ingredients to Use:

- 8 oz. purple cauliflower florets
- 1 tablespoon sugar
- Salt to taste
- 1/2 cup shallots, thinly sliced
- Cooking spray
- 1 lb. Japanese eggplant, cut into 1-inch cubes
- 1/2 cup purple basil leaves
- 1 cup Cherokee purple tomatoes, seeded and chopped
- 1/4 cup red wine vinegar
- 1 oz. kalamata olives, pitted and chopped
- 3 tablespoons capers, drained
- 1/4 cup extra-virgin olive oil

Step Directions

1. In a large bowl, combine the cauliflower, sugar, salt, and shallots. Let stand for 30 minutes.
2. Coat the eggplant cubes with cooking spray, and then spread on oiled grill grates.
3. Set the oven to grill function and the temperature at 350°F.
4. Grill the for 5 to 6 minutes, or until tender.
5. Add the eggplant and the rest of the ingredients to the cauliflower mix.

Serving Suggestion:

Let stand for about 15 minutes before serving.

Tip:

Store in an airtight container and refrigerate for up to a week.

Tofu Steaks with Chimichurri Sauce

These churrasco-style tofu steaks are amazingly meaty, zesty, and herbaceous.

Prep Time and Cooking Time: 45 minutes | Serves: 6

Ingredients to Use:

- 2 tablespoons hemp seeds
- 1 cup fresh parsley leaves
- 1/4 teaspoon red pepper, crushed
- 1 cup fresh cilantro leaves
- 1 garlic clove
- 1 tablespoon red wine vinegar
- 1 tablespoon fresh lime juice
- 1 teaspoon kosher salt, divided
- 2 teaspoons garlic powder
- 1 teaspoon smoked paprika
- 1 teaspoon onion powder
- 1 teaspoon ground cumin
- Salt and pepper to taste
- 1 block extra firm tofu, drained and cut into triangles
- 5 tablespoons extra virgin olive oil, divided
- Cooking spray
- 1/4 teaspoon red pepper, crushed

Step-by-Step Directions

1. Season the tofu triangles with salt, pepper, garlic powder, smoked paprika, onion powder, and cumin.
2. Coat the tofu with cooking spray and arrange on an oiled grill pan.
3. Set the oven on grill mode at medium to high temperature
4. Grill the tofu steaks for 3 to 5 minutes, or until chargrill marks appear.
5. Transfer steaks to a baking sheet.
6. Cook on bake mode at 400°F for 5 minutes.
7. Blend the hemp seeds, parsley, red pepper, cilantro, garlic, vinegar, lime juice, oil, and salt using a food processor.
8. Pour the sauce over the tofu steaks.

Serving Suggestion:

Serve with roasted vegetables and whole grain bread.

Tip:

Drain the tofu by pressing with paper towel.

Roasted Root Traybake

You can't go wrong with these offerings in one tray--crispy, crunchy, soft, zesty and herbaceous.

Prep Time and Cooking Time: 1 hour, 15 minutes | Serves: 4

Ingredients to Use:

- 1kg mixed roots (carrots, parsnips and swede), cut into batons and halved
- 4 thyme sprigs
- 4 rosemary sprigs
- 3 garlic cloves, with skin
- 220g new potatoes, halved
- 2 tablespoon olive oil
- 50g mixed nuts
- 45g feta cheese

Dressing

- 1 lemon, juiced
- 1 cup parsley, finely chopped
- 2 tbsp olive oil

Step-by-Step Directions

1. Combine the roots, herbs, garlic, and potatoes on a grill pan.
2. Drizzle with oil, and then cook on roast mode at 400°F for 10 minutes or until tender.
3. Skin the toasted garlic and whisk together with the rest of the dressing ingredients.
4. Toss the roots in the dressing.

Serving Suggestion:

Top with nuts and feta cheese.

Tip:

You may use vegan cheese instead of feta.

Cheddar Quinoa & Grilled Corn

This creamy recipe is bursting with flavor even with just a few ingredients.

Prep Time and Cooking Time: 30 minutes | Serves: 4

Ingredients to Use:

- 4 ears of sweet corn
- 2 tablespoons olive oil
- 1 cup quinoa, boiled in chicken stock
- 4 oz. cheddar cheese, grated
- 2 tablespoons butter
- 1/4 cup fresh cilantro, chopped
- Salt and pepper to taste

Step-by-Step Directions

1. Brush corn with olive oil and season with salt and pepper.
2. Cover one side of the corn in aluminium oil.
3. Set oven on grill mode at the highest temperature.
4. Grill the corn ears for 10 minutes.
5. Let stand and then remove the kernels from the cob.
6. Heat cooked quinoa in a saucepan with cheese, butter, salt, and pepper.
7. Add in the corn kernels and stir to mix the ingredients.

Serving Suggestion:

Garnish with fresh cilantro.

Tip:

Rotate the corn ears while grilling to cook evenly.

Chapter 9: Snacks

Roasted Shishito Peppers

This recipe will bring summer to your snack time in any time of the year.
Prep Time and Cooking Time: 15 minutes | Serves: 4

Ingredients to Use:

- 2 tablespoons olive oil
- Salt and pepper to taste
- 8 oz Shishito peppers

Step-by-Step Directions

1. Rub the Shishito peppers with olive oil, salt and pepper.
2. Cook on roast setting at 380°F for 5 to 7 minutes.

Serving Suggestion:

Enjoy by itself, or with cornbread.

Tip:

You may also dice them to garnish your salad or soup.

Garlic Carrot Fingers

This recipe balances the sweet and sour flavors of carrots with garlic.
Prep Time and Cooking Time: 22 minutes | Serves: 4

Ingredients to Use:

- 1 lb. carrot, peeled and cut
- 2 teaspoons garlic powder
- Salt and pepper to taste
- 1 tablespoon olive oil

Step-by-Step Directions

1. Coat the carrots by mixing all the ingredients.
2. Set the air fryer oven to roast mode at 390°F.
3. Roast for 10 to 12 minutes.

Serving Suggestion:

Garnish with parsley and cream cheese.

Tip:

If you want a spicy version, just add ground cinnamon and chili powder into the mix.

Roasted Cauliflower

Here's a simple and straightforward recipe that gives you outstanding results.
Prep Time and Cooking Time: 18 minutes | Serves: 4

Ingredients to Use:

- 1 tablespoon sesame oil
- Salt and pepper to taste
- 1 head cauliflower florets
- 3 teaspoons garlic powder

Step-by-Step Directions

1. Season the florets with sesame oil, salt, pepper, and garlic powder.
2. Roast in your air fryer oven at 400°F for 15 minutes.
3. Flip the florets halfway through.

Serving Suggestion:

Garnish with grated parmesan cheese.

Tip:

You may also coat with panko breadcrumbs.

Black Bean Burger

This vegan and oil-free recipe is also a great make-ahead snack.
Prep Time and Cooking Time: 35 minutes |

Serves: 6

Ingredients to Use:

- 16 oz. black beans, drained
- 1/2 cup corn kernels
- 1-1/3 cups rolled oats
- ¾ cup salsa
- 1/2 teaspoon garlic powder
- 1-1/4 teaspoons mild chili powder
- 1/2 teaspoon chipotle chili powder
- 1 tablespoon soy sauce

Step-by-Step Directions

1. Except for the corn, blend all ingredients in a food processor.
2. Add the corn and refrigerate for 15 minutes.
3. Shape the mixture into patties.
4. Set the air fryer oven to bake mode at 375°F.
5. Bake for 15 minutes or until crispy.

Serving Suggestion:

Make a sandwich and serve with guilt-free air fryer fries.

Tip:

Wrap the patties tightly and freeze for up to 3 months.

Spicy Veggie Wontons

This is a better and healthier version of a deep-fried takeout favorite.
Prep Time and Cooking Time: 25 minutes | Serves: 6

Ingredients to Use:

- 30 wonton wrappers
- 1/2 cup carrot, grated and cooked
- 3/4 cup cabbage, grated and cooked
- 1/2 cup mushrooms, finely chopped and cooked
- 1/2 cup white onion, grated and cooked
- 3/4 cup red pepper, finely chopped and cooked
- 1 tablespoon chili sauce
- 1 teaspoon garlic powder
- Salt and pepper to taste
- Cooking spray

Step-by-Step Directions

1. Mix the cooked vegetables with chili sauce, garlic powder, salt and pepper.
2. Stuff the wonton wrappers using the mixture.
3. Spray with olive oil and cook using the air fryer function at 320°F.
4. Cook for 6 minutes or until golden brown.

Serving Suggestion:

Serve with sesame soy or duck sauce for dipping.

Tip:

You may or not preheat your air fryer for at least 3 minutes before putting the wontons in the air fryer basket.

Crispy Falafel

Bring a well-loved street food into your kitchen with this easy recipe.
Prep Time and Cooking Time: 25 minutes | Serves: 6

Ingredients to Use:

- 2 cups dried chickpeas, soaked
- 1 tablespoon chickpea flour
- 3/4 cup parsley, chopped
- 1 medium onion, diced
- 1/4 cup cilantro, chopped
- 2 cloves garlic, minced
- 2 teaspoons ground coriander
- 2 teaspoons cumin powder
- 1/2 teaspoon cayenne pepper
- Salt and pepper to taste

Step-by-Step Directions

1. Pulse all the ingredients in a food processor to make a coarse mixture.
2. Shape the mixture into 1.5-inch balls.
3. Set in a single layer on a lined baking pan.
4. Cook on bake mode at 370°F for 15 minutes or until crispy and golden brown.

Serving Suggestion:

Serve with tzatziki sauce.

Tip:

You may soak the chickpeas overnight for best results.

Roasted Brussels Sprouts

Enjoy the crispy on the outside and tender on the inside with this recipe.

Prep Time and Cooking Time: 17 minutes | Serves: 2

Ingredients to Use:

- 1 tablespoon olive oil
- 10 Brussels sprouts, halved
- Salt and pepper to taste

Step-by-Step Directions

1. Season the Brussels sprouts with olive oil, salt, and pepper.
2. Select the roast function on your air fryer oven.
3. Cook at 360°F for 12 minutes or until lightly browned.

Serving Suggestion:

Drizzle with lime juice and serve with garlic mayo.

Tip:

You may add garlic powder for additional flavor.

Garlic Parmesan Asparagus

This easy recipe packs flavors in an otherwise simple healthy snack.

Prep Time and Cooking Time: 20 minutes | Serves: 4

Ingredients to Use:

- 1 lb. asparagus, trimmed
- 2 teaspoons garlic, minced
- 1/4 cup Parmesan cheese, grated
- 2 tablespoons olive oil
- Salt and pepper to taste

Step-by-Step Directions

1. Coat the asparagus with the rest of the ingredients.
2. Place on the air fryer oven in a single layer.
3. Use the roast function at 400°F for 7 minutes or until cooked as desired.

Serving Suggestion:

Garnish with grated Parmesan cheese.

Tip:

Roast for another minute if you prefer melted cheese.

Roasted Green Beans with Garlic

This tasty low-carb recipe is a perfect keto diet snack.

Prep Time and Cooking Time: 13 minutes | Serves: 4

Ingredients to Use:

- 1 lb. green beans, cut
- 1 teaspoon garlic powder
- 2 tablespoons olive oil
- Salt to taste

Step-by-Step Directions

1. Mix all the ingredients.
2. Spread the green beans on the air fryer tray.

3. Cook on roast mode at 370°F for 4 minutes.
4. Flip and roast for another 4 minutes.

Serving Suggestion:

Grate butter on top and add a squeeze of lemon.

Tip:

Cut the ends and remove the string of the beans.

Zesty Roasted Artichokes

This is an easy recipe that can uplift your mood.
Prep Time and Cooking Time: 22 minutes | Serves: 2

Ingredients to Use:

- 2 tablespoons lemon juice
- 2 tablespoons olive oil
- Salt and pepper to taste
- 2 fresh artichokes, halved

Step-by-Step Directions

1. Combine the lemon juice, olive oil, salt, and pepper in a bowl.
2. Brush the mixture on the artichokes.
3. Set the air fryer oven at 340°F on roast mode.
4. Cook for 9 to 12 minutes.

Serving Suggestion:

Serve with spinach dip.

Tip:

Use freshly squeezed lemon juice.

Baked Corn Nuts

This recipe makes enough for storing a ready-to-eat snack at any time.
Prep Time and Cooking Time: 50 minutes | Serves: 6

Ingredients to Use:

- 1 lb. hominy, dried
- 2 tablespoons olive oil
- 3 tablespoons ranch seasoning
- Salt to taste

Step-by-Step Directions

1. Drizzle olive oil over the kernels.
2. Toss with ranch seasoning and salt.
3. Cook using the bake function of your air fryer oven at 400°F.
4. Bake for 45 minutes or until golden brown.

Serving Suggestion:

Top with Parmesan cheese.

Tip:

Soak the kernels overnight.

Jalapeño Poppers

This recipe makes a satisfyingly filling snack that you will surely love.
Prep Time and Cooking Time: 20 minutes | Serves: 6

Ingredients to Use:

- 4 oz. cream cheese
- 1 cup Monterey Jack cheese
- 1 teaspoon cumin
- 5 jalapeños, cleaned and halved lengthwise
- 5 slices bacon, halved lengthwise
- Olive oil spray

Step-by-Step Directions

1. Combine the cream cheese, cheese, and cumin in a bowl.
2. Fill the jalapeños with the mixture.
3. Wrap a bacon strip around each stuffed jalapeño and secure with a toothpick.
4. Use the air fryer function and set at 370° F.
5. Cook for 6 to 8 minutes, or until the top turns golden brown.

Serving Suggestion:

Serve with ranch dressing.

Tip:

Cook in batches to avoid overcrowding.

Sweet Potato Chips

This simple recipe will cover your next snack attack in a healthier way.

Prep Time and Cooking Time: 20 minutes | Serves: 2

Ingredients to Use:

- 1 large sweet potato, thinly sliced
- 1 teaspoon dried thyme
- 1 tablespoon olive oil
- Salt and pepper to taste

Step-by-Step Directions

1. Toss the sweet potato slices with the rest of the ingredients in a medium bowl.
2. Select the air fryer function on your oven.
3. Cook at 350°F for 14 minutes, or until golden brown.

Serving Suggestion:

Serve hot with ranch sauce for dipping.

Tip:

Use a mandolin slicer to make thinly sliced chips.

Crispy Tacos

Bring Mexican flavors to your home with this simple but amazing recipe.

Prep Time and Cooking Time: 19 minutes | Serves: 6

Ingredients to Use:

- 1 lb. ground turkey, cooked
- 1 pack taco seasoning
- 2 cups lettuce, shredded
- 1/2 cup black beans
- 2 cups Mexican cheese
- 1/2 cup onion, sliced
- 1/2 cup tomatoes, sliced
- 12 hard taco shells

Step-by-Step Directions

1. Mix the taco seasoning with cooked meat.
2. Stuff the taco shells with meat and the rest of the ingredients.
3. Arrange the tacos in the air fryer basket.
4. Cook at 360°F for 4 minutes, or until crispy.

Serving Suggestion:

Serve with salsa.

Tip:

Use a greased foil line to avoid sticking.

Frozen Chicken Fries

You are never too busy to cook this straight from your freezer.

Prep Time and Cooking Time: 8 minutes | Serves: 2

Ingredients to Use:

- 1 pack frozen chicken fries
- 2 tablespoons ketchup

Step-by-Step Directions

1. Place frozen chicken fries in the air fryer basket.
2. Set the oven to air fryer mode at 340°F.
3. Cook for 8 minutes.

Serving Suggestion:

Serve with ketchup or other dipping sauce.

Tip:

Make sure not to overcrowd the air fryer basket.

Zucchini Foil Packets

Here is another take on an all-time favorite grilled vegetable.

Prep Time and Cooking Time: 40 minutes | Serves: 4

Ingredients to Use:

- 2 medium zucchinis, sliced
- 1/4 cup Parmesan cheese, grated
- 1 teaspoon Italian seasoning
- 1 teaspoon dried parsley
- 1 teaspoon dried basil
- 1 teaspoon lemon zest
- 1 teaspoon lemon juice
- 1 tablespoon butter, melted
- 1 tablespoon olive oil

Step-by-Step Directions

1. Combine all ingredients in a bowl.
2. Divide and put the mixture into aluminium foil packets.
3. Set them in the air fryer.
4. Cook on air fryer mode at 350°F for 25 to 30 minutes.

Serving Suggestion:

Top with bits of fresh parsley.

Tip:

You may also use other seasonings of your choice.

Fried Pickles with Ranch Dip

This oil-free recipe will get pickle fans excited.

Prep Time and Cooking Time: 55 minutes | Serves: 3

Ingredients to Use:

- 1/2 cup breadcrumbs
- 1/4 cup Parmesan cheese, grated
- 1 teaspoon garlic powder
- 1 teaspoon dried oregano
- 1 egg, whisked with 1 tablespoon water
- 2 cups dill pickle slices, dried
- 2 tablespoons ranch, for dipping

Step-by-Step Directions

1. Combine the breadcrumbs, cheese, garlic powder, and oregano in a bowl.
2. Dip each pickle chip in egg and then coat with the mixture.
3. Cook on air fryer setting at 400°F for 10 minutes.

Serving Suggestion:

Serve immediately with ranch dip.

Tip:

Do not overlap when placing in the air fryer.

Cheesy Tortellini Bites

This snack only takes a few minutes using your air fryer oven!

Prep Time and Cooking Time: 25 minutes | Serves: 6

Ingredients to Use:

- 2 large eggs, beaten
- 1 cup all-purpose flour
- 1 cup Panko breadcrumbs
- 1/3 cup Parmesan cheese, grated
- 1/2 teaspoon crushed red pepper flakes
- 1 teaspoon dried oregano
- 1/2 teaspoon garlic powder
- Salt and pepper to taste
- 9 oz. cheese tortellini, cooked
- 2 tablespoons marinara, for dipping

Step-by-Step Directions

1. Create a mixture of breadcrumbs, cheese, pepper flakes, oregano, garlic powder, salt and pepper.
2. Coat the tortellini in flour, dip in eggs, and then coat with the Panko mixture.
3. Air fry at 370°F for 10 minutes.

Serving Suggestion:

Serve warm with marinara sauce.

Tip:

Pair with a red wine mule, if available.

Vegan Pakoras

Travel to the origin of this fried snack with this air fryer recipe.
Prep Time and Cooking Time: 30 minutes | Serves: 4

Ingredients to Use:

- 1 cup cauliflower, chopped
- 1/2 cup yellow potatoes, chopped
- 1/2 clove garlic, minced
- 1/4 red onion, chopped
- 1/2 teaspoon curry powder
- 1/4 teaspoon cumin
- 2/3 tablespoons chickpea flour
- 1/3 tablespoons water
- 1/2 teaspoon coriander
- Salt and cayenne pepper to taste
- Cooking spray

Step-by-Step Directions

1. Mix all the ingredients in a large bowl. Let it sit for 10 minutes.
2. Scoop 2 tablespoons of the mixture on the air fryer basket, and then flatten. Repeat without overcrowding the basket.
3. Spritz with cooking spray.
4. Air fry at 350°F for 16 minutes, flipping halfway through.

Serving Suggestion:

Serve with vegan yogurt for dipping.

Tip:

You may also use regular yogurt if you are not vegan.

Green Plantain Chips

Make plantain chips without any hassle using this recipe.
Prep Time and Cooking Time: 20 minutes | Serves: 2

Ingredients to Use:

- Avocado oil spray
- 1 green plantain, cut into strips
- Salt to taste

Step-by-Step Directions

1. Spray the air fryer basket and the plantain strips with avocado oil.
2. Arrange in the basket without overlapping.
3. Cook on air fryer setting at 350°F for 10 to 15 minutes, flipping with tongs halfway through.

Serving Suggestion:

Sprinkle with sugar.

Tip:

Use a vegetable peeler to make thin chips.

Chapter 10: Cakes, Cookies & Muffins

Upside Down Pineapple Cake

This sweet dessert will surely give everyone a festive mood.

Prep Time and Cooking Time: 40 minutes | Serves: 6

Ingredients to Use:

- 1/4 cup brown sugar
- 1 package yellow cake mix
- 2 tablespoons melted butter
- 2-3 maraschino cherries
- 20 oz. can pineapple slices
- Ingredients needed to make cake mix

Step-by-Step Directions

1. Spray the bottom of the baking pan with non-stick spray.
2. Melt butter in the microwave and pour it on the baking pan bottom.
3. Next, sprinkle brown sugar on top of melted butter.
4. Put the pineapples on top of the sugar.
5. Add cherries in the pineapple holes.
6. Follow the instructions on the cake mix box to make the batter.
7. Pour batter in the pan on top of pineapples.
8. Choose the bake function.
9. Bake for 25 minutes at 320°F.

Serving Suggestion:

Let the cake cool down before flipping the pan.

Tip:

Check the middle with a toothpick to see if the cake is done cooking. The ingredients will vary depending on the cake mix package you will use.

Easiest Air Fryer Brownies

Make air fryer brownies that are crisp on the outside and soft and moist on the inside.

Prep Time and Cooking Time: 20 minutes | Serves: 4

Ingredients to Use:

- 2 large eggs
- 1/4 teaspoon baking powder
- 1/2 cup all-purpose flour
- 1/4 cup unsalted butter, melted
- 6 tablespoons unsweetened cocoa powder
- 1/2 teaspoon vanilla extract
- 3/4 cup sugar
- 1 tablespoon vegetable oil
- 1/4 teaspoon salt

Step-by-Step Directions

1. Grease a 7-inch baking pan. Set aside.
2. Preheat air fryer to 330°F.
3. Combine all the ingredients in a large bowl and mix well.
4. Gently pour into pan.
5. Choose the bake function.
6. Bake for 15 minutes in the air fryer.

Serving Suggestion:

Let the brownie cool down before slicing and serving.

Tip:

Garnish with powdered sugar.

Oatmeal & Chocolate Chip Cookies

This big batch of chewy cookies is perfect for a big family or for sharing with friends.

Prep Time and Cooking Time: 40 minutes | Serves: 20

Ingredients to Use:

- 1 cup nuts, chopped
- 1 cup softened butter
- 2 cups semi-sweet chocolate chips
- 3/4 cup sugar
- 1 teaspoon salt
- 3/4 cup packed brown sugar
- 1 teaspoon baking soda
- 2 large room temperature eggs
- 1 teaspoon vanilla extract
- 1 package instant vanilla pudding mix
- 3 cups quick-cooking oats
- 1-1/2 cups all-purpose flour

Step-by-Step Directions

1. Preheat air fryer to 325°F.
2. Combine sugars and butter and whisk until fluffy.
3. Add eggs and vanilla extract.
4. In a separate bowl, combine pudding mix, oats, flour, salt, and baking soda.
5. Gradually add dry ingredients to the first bowl of fluffy cream mixture.
6. Fold in nuts and chocolate chips.
7. Using a spoon, scoop and drop dough into a greased baking tray.
8. Slightly flatten the top to create a cookie shape.
9. Arrange cookies at least 1 inch apart.
10. Choose the air fry function.
11. Air fry for 8-10 minutes or until the edges turn brown.

Serving Suggestion:

Remove from tray and let cookies cool on a wire rack before serving.

Tip:

Make sure that all ingredients are cold so the biscuit shape can hold up. These biscuits can be made ahead and stored in the freezer.

Banana, Peanut Butter, & Oatmeal Air Fryer Cookies

Chewy and chunky cookies with cranberry bits in every bite.

Prep Time and Cooking Time: 15 minutes | Serves: 6

Ingredients to Use:

- 1/2 cup whole wheat flour
- 1/2 cup chunky peanut butter
- 2 teaspoons ground cinnamon
- 1/4 teaspoon baking soda
- 1/4 cup non-fat milk powder
- 1 cup ripe banana, mashed
- 1 cup dried raisins or cranberries
- 1/2 teaspoon vanilla extract
- 1/2 cup honey
- 1 cup old-fashioned oats
- 1/2 teaspoon salt

Step-by-Step Directions

1. Preheat air fryer to 300°F.
2. Combine honey, peanut butter, banana, and vanilla extract in a bowl.
3. in a separate bowl, mix milk, flour, oats, baking soda, salt, and cinnamon.
4. Slowly add and mix flour mixture to the bowl with banana.
5. Add dried cranberries.
6. Grease baking tray.
7. Scoop 1/4 cup of batter and arrange in the tray with 2 inches of space apart.
8. Slightly flatten to achieve cookie shape.
9. Choose the air fry function.
10. Air fry for 7 minutes.

Serving Suggestion:

Let cookies cool down for 1 minute before serving.

Tip:

You can freeze the cookies and reheat them in the air fryer at 300°F.

Classic Chocolate Chip Cookies

This is a crowd favorite that will only take under 15 minutes to make in an air fryer.
Prep Time and Cooking Time: 13 minutes | Serves: 18

Ingredients to Use:

- 2 cups semi-sweet chocolate chips
- 1 teaspoon vanilla extract
- 1 teaspoon baking soda
- 1/2 cup unsalted butter
- 1 egg
- 1/2 cup brown sugar
- 1/4 cup white sugar
- 1/2 teaspoon almond extract
- 1-1/2 cups all-purpose flour
- 1/2 teaspoon salt

Step-by-Step Directions

1. Soften butter in a microwave oven. It should be partially melted but not completely.
2. Mix in the sugars.
3. Add vanilla extract and egg. Mix.
4. Add the dry ingredients followed by the chocolate chips. Stir gently.
5. Form into 2-inch balls.
6. Line air fryer basket with parchment paper.
7. Choose bake function.
8. Arrange cookies and bake for 8 minutes at 300°F.

Serving Suggestion:

Let cookies cool down for 4 minutes before removing from the air fryer.

Tip:

Use an egg that is within room temperature to get the best results. You can refrigerate the dough for an hour to make it easier to form into cookie shapes.

Chocolate Applesauce Ramekin Cookies

This cake recipe makes a lovely dessert for two in under 30 minutes.
Prep Time and Cooking Time: 25 minutes | Serves: 2

Ingredients to Use:

- 1/4 teaspoon baking powder
- 1/8 teaspoon salt
- 2 tablespoons sugar
- 1/8 teaspoon baking soda
- 2 tablespoons mini chocolate chips
- 2 tablespoons milk
- 1/4 cup flour
- 1/4 teaspoon vanilla
- 2 tablespoon applesauce
- 1 tablespoon melted butter

Step-by-Step Directions

1. In a large bowl, combine flour, baking soda, baking powder, sugar, and salt.
2. Make a crater in the middle and add butter, applesauce, and vanilla.
3. Mix and add the chocolate chips.
4. Grease ramekins.
5. Choose the bake function.
6. Pour batter in ramekins and bake for 15 minutes at 375°F.

Serving Suggestion:

Let ramekins cool and serve with a scoop of vanilla ice cream.

Tip:

Garnish with mint leaves.

Soft &Chewy Air Fryer Molasses Cookies

These deliciously sweet cookies have a hint of spicy ginger and a soft and chewy center.

Prep Time and Cooking Time: 15 minutes | Serves: 15

Ingredients to Use:

- 2 teaspoon ground cinnamon
- 1-1/2 teaspoon Celtic sea salt
- 1-1/2 cups softened butter
- 1 cup brown sugar
- 1/4 cup granulated sugar
- 4 teaspoons baking soda
- 1/2 cup molasses
- 4 cups all-purpose flour
- 1 teaspoon ground cloves
- 2 eggs
- 1 teaspoon ground ginger

Step-by-Step Directions

1. Ina bowl, mix salt, ginger, flour, cloves, cinnamon, and baking soda.
2. In a separate bowl, combine sugar and butter until fluffy using a mixer at a medium setting.
3. Add molasses and eggs with a low setting.
4. Add the dry ingredients. Mix well.
5. Make 1-inch balls from the dough.
6. Roll the balls into the granulated sugar and coat each piece completely.
7. Arrange dough in a baking tray with 1 inch of space in between.
8. Choose the air fry function.
9. Air fry for 8-10 minutes at 375°F.

Serving Suggestion:

Cool for 2 minutes before removing from tray.

Tip:

The center is meant to be gooey. If the edges are firm, the cookies are ready. Cookies may be stored in an airtight cookie jar and will last for a week.

Air Fried Oreo Cookies

A 3-ingredient cookie recipe that will surely delight Oreo lovers.

Prep Time and Cooking Time: 14 minutes | Serves: 6

Ingredients to Use:

- 1 tablespoon melted butter
- 12 pieces Oreo cookies
- 1 sheet puff pastry

Step-by-Step Directions

1. Roll out puff pastry on a flat surface.
2. Put a cookie on top of the dough and cut a circle big enough to wrap the cookie.
3. Wrap all cookies with dough and brush melted butter on the surface.
4. Choose the air fry function.
5. Air fry for 12 minutes at 350°F.
6. Turn cookies halfway to brown evenly.

Serving Suggestion:

Plate and sprinkle powdered sugar on top.

Tip:

You can store the cookies in the fridge and reheat them in the air fryer for a few minutes.

Air Fryer Red Velvet Cookies

A cookie version of the red velvet cake that we love.

Prep Time and Cooking Time: 20 minutes | Serves: 10

Ingredients to Use:

- 2 eggs
- 8 oz. softened butter
- 1/4 cup milk
- 8 oz. softened cream cheese
- 1 package cake mix red velvet
- 1/2 cup powdered sugar

Step-by-Step Directions

1. Preheat air fryer to 350°F.
2. Combine butter and cream cheese using

a mixer.
3. Add the eggs and mix.
4. Add the cake mix and milk until creamy and soft.
5. Create balls and roll them in powdered sugar.
6. Arrange cookies in a lined baking tray.
7. Choose the air fry function.
8. Air fry for 10-15 minutes.

Serving Suggestion:

Serve while still warm with a glass of milk.

Tip:

Monitor the baking closely as time may vary depending on the type of air fryer used. Cookies are done if the center has set.

Oatmeal Caramel Cookie Bar

A giant crumbly cookie best shared with friends and family.
Prep Time and Cooking Time: 20 minutes | Serves: 10

Ingredients to Use:

- 1 cup old fashioned oats
- 1/2 cup sea salt caramel chips
- 1 cup whole wheat flour
- 1 large egg
- 1/2 teaspoon baking soda
- 1/4 cup milk
- 1/4 teaspoon salt
- 2 tablespoons melted butter
- 1/3 cup brown sugar
- 1 teaspoon vanilla extract

Step-by-Step Directions

1. Combine flour, salt, oats, and baking soda in a bowl. Set aside.
2. Mix egg, brown sugar, butter, milk, and vanilla in a separate bowl.
3. Preheat air fryer to 330°F.
4. Slowly add the dry ingredients to the wet ingredients until fully combined.
5. Add caramel chips.
6. Line tray with parchment paper.
7. Put the dough in the tray and smoothen the top with a spatula.
8. Choose the bake function.
9. Bake for 15 minutes or until the surface turns brown.

Serving Suggestion:

Let the cookie cool for a few minutes before serving. Slice or break into smaller pieces.

Tip:

You may use a toothpick to check if the cookie is done. These cookies may be stored in an airtight container for 5 days or refrigerated for up to 3 months.

Easy Peanut Butter Cookies

This 10-minute recipe is perfect for a quick treat for the kids and those who are still kids at heart.
Prep Time and Cooking Time: 10 minutes | Serves: 8

Ingredients to Use:

- 1 cup sugar
- 1 cup peanut butter
- 1 egg

Step-by-Step Directions

1. Mix all ingredients in a bowl until well combined.
2. Line tray with parchment paper.
3. Using an ice cream scoop or spoon, arrange the dough in the tray.
4. Use a fork to flatten the top.
5. Choose the air fry function.
6. Air fry for 5 minutes at 350°F.

Serving Suggestion:

Serve with coffee, tea, or milk.

Tip:

Make a big batch and store it in airtight containers.

Air Fried Nutella Cookies

This is a simple cookie recipe that uses ingredients you already have in your pantry.
Prep Time and Cooking Time: 14 minutes | Serves: 10

Ingredients to Use:

- 1 cup flour
- 1-1/4 cup Nutella
- 2 large eggs

Step-by-Step Directions

1. In a large mixing bowl, mix all ingredients until well blended.
2. Line baking tray with parchment paper.
3. Use an ice cream scoop or large spoon and arrange cookies in the tray.
4. Choose the air fry function.
5. Air fry for 4 minutes at 340°F.

Serving Suggestion:

Sprinkle some powdered sugar on top and serve.

Tip:

These cookies can be stored in airtight containers and will last for a few days.

French Vanilla Cookies

This 3-ingredient cookie recipe only takes 10 minutes to make.
Prep Time and Cooking Time: 10 minutes | Serves: 12

Ingredients to Use:

- 2 large eggs
- 1/4 cup vegetable oil
- 1 package cake mix French Vanilla flavor

Step-by-Step Directions

1. Whisk all the ingredients in a bowl.
2. Spray or coat tray with oil.
3. Arrange cookies leaving at least 2 inches of space in between.
4. Using a fork, slightly flatten the surface.
5. Choose the air fry function.
6. Air fry for 5 minutes at 350°F.

Serving Suggestion:

Sprinkle some sugar on top and serve.

Tip:

You may use any flavor of cake mix for this recipe. You may substitute canola with vegetable oil.

Air Fryer Blueberry Cookies

Lovely cookies to eat as a dessert or paired with your morning coffee or tea.
Prep Time and Cooking Time: 9 minutes | Serves: 4

Ingredients to Use:

- 1 tablespoon melted butter
- 1 teaspoon vanilla extract
- 1 package Jiffy blueberry muffin mix
- 1 large egg

Step-by-Step Directions

1. Combine muffin mix, vanilla extract, egg, and butter.
2. Scoop dough and arrange in greased baking trays.
3. Choose the air fry function.
4. Air fry for 4 minutes at 320°F.

Serving Suggestion:

Cookies are ready once the edges turn brown. Plate and serve with your beverage of choice.

Tip:

You can make a big batch to store in airtight containers or the fridge.

Milo Krispies Cookies

This recipe yields exquisite-looking cookies

that are hard to resist.
Prep Time and Cooking Time: 20 minutes | Serves: 5

Ingredients to Use:

- 1/3 cup butter
- 1 tablespoon corn flour
- 2 oz. milk or dark chocolate pieces
- 13-in-1 Milo packet
- 1/3 cup sugar
- 1 cup flour
- 3 cups rice krispies or puffs

Step-by-Step Directions

1. Preheat air fryer to 338°F.
2. Mix sugar and butter until fluffy.
3. Add flour and Milo.
4. Form into balls and flatten into cookie shapes.
5. Coat with rice puffs.
6. Line tray or basket with foil.
7. Arrange cookies in the tray.
8. Choose the bake function.
9. Bake for 12 minutes.

Serving Suggestion:

Drizzle melted chocolate on top and serve.

Tip:

Make sure that you leave some space in between the cookies before baking.

Fluffy Bran Muffins

This muffin recipe is not only tasty but is also great for digestion.
Prep Time and Cooking Time: 35 minutes | Serves: 8

Ingredients to Use:

- 1 cup all-purpose flour
- 1/3 cup unsweetened applesauce
- 1 teaspoon salt
- 1 teaspoon baking powder
- 1-1/2 cups Fiber One cereal
- 1 egg
- 1 teaspoon vanilla
- 2/3 cup brown sugar
- 1 teaspoon baking soda
- 1 cup buttermilk

Step-by-Step Directions

1. Combine buttermilk and cereal in a mixing bowl. Set aside for 20 minutes.
2. Combine all the wet ingredients in a separate bowl.
3. In another bowl, combine the dry ingredients.
4. Combine all three mixtures in a large bowl and mix well.
5. Coat muffin tins with non-stick cooking spray.
6. Fill muffin tins up to 2/3 full with batter.
7. Choose the air fry function.
8. Air fry for 12-15 minutes at 320°F.

Serving Suggestion:

Plate and serve with butter.

Tip:

Make this recipe for family members that have trouble with indigestion.

Easy Blueberry Streusel muffins

These wonderfully filling muffins are great for breakfast with your favorite beverage.
Prep Time and Cooking Time: 24 minutes | Serves: 12

Ingredients to Use:

- 1/2 cup fresh blueberries
- 2 eggs
- 1 cup flour plus 4 tablespoons for topping
- 1 teaspoon baking powder
- 1/3 cup milk
- 1 tablespoon vanilla
- 2 tablespoons sugar plus 4 tablespoons for topping

- 3 tablespoons melted butter
- 4 tablespoons butter for topping
- 4 tablespoons brown sugar

Step-by-Step Directions

1. Combine flour, baking powder, and sugar in a mixing bowl.
2. Add the milk, melted butter, eggs, and vanilla extract.
3. Add fresh blueberries.
4. To create topping, mix brown sugar, 4 tablespoons sugar, 4 tablespoons butter, and 4 tablespoons flour.
5. Pour batter into greased or lined muffin tins about 2/3 full.
6. Add the topping over the batter.
7. Choose the bake function.
8. Bake for 12-14 minutes at 320°F.

Serving Suggestion:

Garnish with fresh berries.

Tip:

These will last for 2-3 days in airtight containers at room temperature.

Pumpkin Muffins with Cream Cheese Frosting

This is a neat recipe to try if you love pumpkin. Pair these delicious muffins with pumpkin spice latte too.

Prep Time and Cooking Time: 35 minutes | Serves: 8

Ingredients to Use:

- 1 cup canned pumpkin
- 1-1/2 cups all-purpose flour
- 1 teaspoon pumpkin pie spice
- 2 eggs
- 1 teaspoon baking powder
- 1-/4 cup sugar
- 1 teaspoon baking soda
- 1/3 cup vegetable oil
- 1 teaspoon ground cinnamon
- 1 teaspoon salt plus ½ teaspoon for frosting
- 1/2 cup unsalted butter, room temperature
- 4 cups powdered sugar
- 8 oz. cream cheese, room temperature
- 1 teaspoon vanilla extract

Step-by-Step Directions

1. Combine eggs, 1-1/4 cup sugar, and vegetable oil in a bowl.
2. In a separate bowl, mix baking powder, soda, flour, cinnamon, pumpkin spice, and 1 teaspoon salt.
3. Combine both mixtures and mix well.
4. Pour batter into lined or greased muffin tins about 2/3 full.
5. Choose the bake function.
6. Bake for 10-12 minutes at 320°F.
7. To make the frosting, combine unsalted butter, cream cheese, vanilla, 1/2 teaspoon salt, and powdered sugar in a mixing bowl.

Serving Suggestion:

Muffins need to cool completely before adding the frosting.

Tip:

Sprinkle with pumpkin spice powder or sprinkles.

Orange & Cranberry Muffins

This is a great recipe to make if you have plenty of fresh cranberries available.

Prep Time and Cooking Time: 32 minutes | Serves: 8

Ingredients to Use:

- 1 teaspoon lemon zest, grated
- 2 tablespoons orange zest
- 1 teaspoon grated orange zest
- 1 cup diced cranberries
- 1/3 cup vegetable oil

- 8 tablespoons sugar
- 3/4 cup milk
- 1-3/4 cup flour
- 1 large egg
- 1/2 teaspoon salt
- 3 teaspoons baking powder

Step-by-Step Directions

1. Put cranberries in a bowl.
2. Add 2 tablespoons sugar and orange zest. Mix well.
3. In a separate bowl, mix the remaining sugar, flour, salt, and baking powder.
4. Add egg, oil, and milk. Mix until everything is well combined.
5. Add cranberries, lemon zest, and orange zest.
6. Fill greased muffin tin with batter.
7. Choose the bake function.
8. Bake in the air fryer at 325°F for 15 minutes.

Serving Suggestion:

Let muffins cool for a few minutes before serving.

Tip:

Use a toothpick to tell if muffins are ready.

Double Choco Chip Muffins

These chocolate loaded muffins are not only toothsome, but incredibly moist as well.

Prep Time and Cooking Time: 35 minutes | Serves: 12

Ingredients to Use:

- 2 teaspoons vanilla extract
- 1/2 cup unsweetened cocoa powder
- 1-1/4 cup all-purpose flour
- 1 cup bittersweet chocolate chips
- 1 tablespoon vegetable oil
- 3/4 cup milk
- 1 teaspoon baking powder
- 1 teaspoon baking soda
- 1/2 cup brown sugar
- 2 eggs
- 1 teaspoon salt
- 4 tablespoons melted unsalted butter

Step-by-Step Directions

1. Combine cocoa, chocolate chips, flour, baking soda, salt, and baking powder in a bowl and mix well.
2. Add eggs, melted butter, milk, brown sugar, vanilla extract, and vegetable oil. Mix until well combined.
3. Coat muffin tins with non-stick cooking spray.
4. Fill with batter about 2/3 full.
5. Sprinkle sugar on top.
6. Choose the air fry function.
7. Air fry for 12-15 minutes at 320°F.

Serving Suggestion:

Sprinkle with powdered sugar and serve.

Tip:

You may also use silicone muffin cups for this recipe.

Air Fryer Apple Muffins

This air fryer recipe is a perfect way to use fresh apples while they are in season.

Prep Time and Cooking Time: 24 minutes | Serves: 2

Ingredients to Use:

- 1/2 cup apples, diced
- 1/2 teaspoon salt
- 1/2 cup all-purpose flour plus 4 tablespoons for topping
- 2 tablespoons melted butter
- 3 tablespoons butter for topping
- 1 teaspoon ground cinnamon plus 1 teaspoon for topping
- 3 tablespoons heavy cream
- 1 egg yolk
- 1 teaspoon baking powder

- 3 tablespoons brown sugar plus 4 tablespoons for topping
- 1 teaspoon vanilla extract

Step-by-Step Directions

1. Combine 1 teaspoon cinnamon, 3 tablespoons sugar, ½ cup flour, salt, and baking powder in a bowl.
2. Next add the cream, egg, melted butter, and vanilla. Mix well.
3. Fold in apples.
4. To make the topping, combine 4 tablespoons flour, 1 teaspoon cinnamon, and 4 tablespoons brown sugar.
5. Pour batter into greased ramekins.
6. Sprinkle topping on batter.
7. Choose the air fry function.
8. Air fry for 320°F for 12-14 minutes.

Serving Suggestion:

Let muffins cool for a few minutes before serving.

Tip:

You can tweak this recipe to include ingredients you love. Try adding some frosting or nuts.

Easy Cornmeal Muffins

This super easy to make muffin is perfect as a side dish for your savory dishes.
Prep Time and Cooking Time: 17 minutes | Serves: 12

Ingredients to Use:

- 1/3 cup vegetable oil
- 1 cup flour
- 1/4 cup sugar
- 1 cup yellow cornmeal
- 2 large eggs
- 1 teaspoon salt
- 1 teaspoon baking soda
- 1-1/4 cups buttermilk
- 1 tablespoon baking powder

Step-by-Step Directions

1. Combine cornmeal, salt, baking soda, baking powder, sugar, and flour.
2. Add the oil, eggs, and buttermilk. Mix well.
3. Pour batter into greased or lined muffin trays.
4. Fill muffin cups about 2/3 full.
5. Choose the bake function.
6. Bake for 12 minutes at 330°F.

Serving Suggestion:

Serve while still warm and with a slice of butter on top.

Tip:

Leftover muffins can be refrigerated and quickly reheated in the air fryer.

Banana Walnut Muffins

This muffin recipe is a great way to save very ripe bananas from ending up in the bin.
Prep Time and Cooking Time: 22 minutes | Serves: 6

Ingredients to Use:

- 1 cup walnuts, chopped
- 3 ripe bananas
- 1-1/2 cups flour
- 1/3 cup melted butter
- 1/2 teaspoon salt
- 3/4 cup sugar
- 1/4 teaspoon ground cinnamon
- 1 teaspoon baking soda
- 1 teaspoon vanilla extract
- 1 teaspoon baking powder
- 1 egg

Step-by-Step Directions

1. In a large bowl, mix flour, cinnamon, bananas, sugar, butter, egg, baking soda, vanilla, and baking powder until smooth.
2. Add walnuts.
3. Pour batter into greased muffin trays.

4. Choose the bake function.
5. Bake in the air fryer at 320°F for 12 minutes.

Serving Suggestion:

Top with frosting or a sprinkle of powdered sugar.

Tip:

Use non-stick cooking spray to grease muffin trays. Once the 12 minutes are up, check if muffins are ready. Add a minute or two until muffins are done.

Bacon & Cheese Savory Muffins

These savory muffins are excellent snacks or even meal-replacements while on the go.
Prep Time and Cooking Time: 22 minutes | Serves: 6

Ingredients to Use:

- 2 tablespoons olive oil
- 1 cup cheddar cheese, shredded
- 1 cup milk
- 2-1/2 cups all-purpose flour
- 2 teaspoons baking powder
- 1 egg
- 1 teaspoon dried basil
- 1/4 cup cooked bacon, crumbled
- 1/2 teaspoon salt

Step-by-Step Directions

1. In a mixing bowl, combine cheese, basil, salt, flour, and baking powder.
2. Add egg, olive oil, milk, and bacon. Mix well.
3. Fill a greased muffin tray with batter up to 2/3's full.
4. Choose the bake function.
5. Bake for 15 minutes at 350°F.

Serving Suggestion:

Let the tray cool before taking out the muffins. Plate and serve.

Tip:

Exercise caution when taking out the muffin tray. After 15 minutes of baking, check for doneness using a toothpick. If the toothpick comes out clean, the muffins are ready.

Lemon & Blueberry Muffins

This recipe highlights the zesty and sweet flavors of lemon and blueberries.
Prep Time and Cooking Time: 24 minutes | Serves: 5

Ingredients to Use:

- 2 tablespoons lemon juice
- 1 cup flour
- 1/4 cup butter
- 1/2 cup sugar
- 1/2 teaspoon salt
- 1/4 cup milk
- 1/2 cup blueberries
- 1 teaspoon baking powder
- 1 teaspoon vanilla
- 1 tablespoon lemon zest
- 1 egg

Step-by-Step Directions

1. Spray a muffin tray with non-stick cooking spray.
2. In a large mixing bowl, mix all the ingredients until fully combined.
3. Pour batter into muffin cups up to ¾ full.
4. Choose the bake function.
5. Bake for 14 minutes at 320°F.

Serving Suggestion:

Let the muffins slightly cool before serving. Garnish with fresh blueberries and mint leaves.

Tip:

Make a big batch and store in Ziploc bags in

the fridge. Reheat anytime in the air fryer for a few minutes.

Spaghetti & Meatball Muffins

This savory muffin recipe is the perfect lunchbox treat for pasta lovers.
Prep Time and Cooking Time: 21 minutes | Serves: 24

Ingredients to Use:

- 1 egg slightly beaten
- 8.8 oz. cooked pasta
- 2 cups mozzarella cheese, shredded
- 2 cups pasta sauce
- 24 cooked meatballs
- 1/2 cup parmesan cheese, shredded

Step-by-Step Directions

1. Put the cooked pasta in a bowl and add 1 1/2 cup of pasta sauce.
2. Add egg and stir.
3. Add 1 cup of the mozzarella cheese and 1/2 cup parmesan cheese. Mix well.
4. Fill each muffin cup with the pasta.
5. Choose the air fry function.
6. Air fry for 4-5 minutes at 390°F.
7. Put a meatball on top and push it into the center.
8. Add some more pasta sauce and mozzarella on top.
9. Air fry for 2 minutes more with the same air fryer settings until cheese melts.

Serving Suggestion:

Let muffins cool down before serving.

Tip:

Be careful when taking out the muffin cups to add the meatballs. Use silicone-tipped tongs. These muffins can be stored in the fridge and reheated in the air fryer.

Cheesy Tuna Melt

Try this savory muffin recipe when you get hungry and have little time to spare for preparation.
Prep Time and Cooking Time: 22 minutes | Serves: 4

Ingredients to Use:

- 1 tablespoon Dijon mustard
- 3/4 cup packaged coleslaw mix
- 2 cans white tuna chunks, drained
- 1/2 cup shredded cheese
- 1/2 teaspoon dried dill
- 3 tablespoon mayonnaise
- 3 green onions sliced
- 4 English muffins, halved

Step-by-Step Directions

1. Preheat air fryer to 370°F.
2. In a bowl, combine coleslaw mix, green onion, and tuna.
3. In a separate bowl, mix mustard, mayonnaise, and dill.
4. Add mixture to the bowl with tuna and mix well.
5. Put 2 tablespoons of the tuna mixture on top of the halved muffin.
6. Choose the air fry function.
7. Air fry for 3-4 minutes.
8. Add the cheese on top and air fry for another 1-2 minutes.

Serving Suggestion:

Let the muffins cool down for a few minutes before serving as melted cheese can burn.

Tip:

Garnish with basil or dill.

Chapter 11: Appetizer Recipes

Dry Rubbed Chicken Wings

There's nothing like this dry rubbed chicken wings to make your guests go wow.
Prep Time and Cooking Time: 45 minutes | Serves: 6

Ingredients to Use:

- 2 lb. chicken wings
- 2 tablespoons olive oil

Dry rub

- 1 tablespoon brown sugar
- 1 teaspoon garlic powder
- 1 teaspoon smoked paprika
- 1 teaspoon chili powder
- 1 teaspoon onion powder
- 1 teaspoon dried mustard powder
- 1 teaspoon cumin
- 1 teaspoon paprika
- 1/2 teaspoon oregano
- 1/2 teaspoon ground thyme
- Pinch cayenne pepper
- Salt and pepper to taste

Step-by-Step Directions

1. Combine the dry rub ingredients in a bowl.
2. In another bowl, toss wings in oil.
3. Sprinkle all sides with the dry rub.
4. Place inside the air fryer oven.
5. Choose bake function.
6. Bake at 370 degrees F for 8 to 10 minutes per side.

Serving Suggestion:

Garnish with lettuce leaves and cucumber slices.

Tip:

Thaw first if you are using frozen chicken wings.

Chili Cheese Fries

Top your fries with chili and cheese, and serve as appetizer to your guests.
Prep Time and Cooking Time: 20 minutes | Serves: 6

Ingredients to Use:

- 1 pack French fries
- Salt and pepper to taste
- 15 oz. chili
- 1/2 cup cheddar cheese, shredded

Step-by-Step Directions

1. Spread the fries in the air crisper tray.
2. Choose air fry setting in your air fryer oven.
3. Cook at 400 degrees F for 7 to 8 minutes, stirring once or twice.
4. In a pan over medium heat, warm up the chili.
5. Top the fries with the chili.
6. Sprinkle with cheese.
7. Place in the air fryer oven.
8. Choose bake setting.
9. Bake at 350 degrees F for 3 minutes or until cheese has melted.

Serving Suggestion:

Top with a dollop of sour cream.

Tip:

You can also use homemade potato fries for this recipe.

Baked Potato Rounds

These baked potato rounds will definitely be

the highlight of the party.
Prep Time and Cooking Time: 30 minutes | Serves: 8

Ingredients to Use:

- 2 potatoes, sliced into ½ inch thick rounds
- Cooking spray
- Salt and pepper to taste
- 1 cup sour cream
- 1 cup cheddar cheese, shredded

Step-by-Step Directions

1. Spray potato rounds with oil.
2. Sprinkle with salt and pepper.
3. Add the potato rounds to the air crisper tray.
4. Select air fry setting.
5. Cook at 370 degrees F for 15 minutes, flipping once.
6. Let cool.
7. Top with sour cream and cheddar cheese.
8. Put these back to the air fryer oven.
9. Choose bake setting.
10. Bake at 350 degrees F for 3 minutes or until cheese has melted.

Serving Suggestion:

Sprinkle with dried herbs.

Tip:

Use Russet potatoes for this recipe.

Mediterranean Nachos

This kind of appetizer will certainly make you look like a kitchen pro.
Prep Time and Cooking Time: 20 minutes | Serves: 8

Ingredients to Use:

- 10 corn tortillas
- 4 tablespoons olive oil
- Salt to taste

Toppings

- 2 cups cooked pulled pork
- 1 cup cucumbers, chopped
- 1 cup tomatoes, chopped
- 1/2 cup black olives, pitted and sliced
- 1/2 cup feta cheese
- 1/2 cup tzatziki sauce
- Fresh dill

Step-by-Step Directions

1. Slice tortillas into wedges.
2. Coat with olive oil and sprinkle with salt.
3. Arrange in a single layer in the air crisper tray.
4. Set it to air fry.
5. Cook at 320 degrees F for 1 to 2 minutes per side.
6. Let cool and transfer to a serving platter.
7. Sprinkle all the toppings on top of the chips.

Serving Suggestion:

Drizzle with hot pepper sauce.

Tip:

You can also use tortilla chips for this recipe.

Teriyaki Beef Skewers

If you want something heavy for your appetizers, here's a recipe you should consider.
Prep Time and Cooking Time: 6 hours and 30 minutes | Serves: 8

Ingredients to Use:

- 3 cups brown sugar
- 2 cups soy sauce
- 1 cup pineapple juice
- 1 cup water
- 2 teaspoons garlic powder
- 1/2 cup vegetable oil
- 2 lb. steak, sliced

Step-by-Step Directions

1. Toss all the ingredients in a bowl.
2. Coat the steak slices evenly with the marinade.
3. Cover and marinate for 6 hours in the refrigerator.
4. Thread beef onto skewers.
5. Place inside the air fryer oven.
6. Set it to grill.
7. Cook at 400 degrees F for 5 to 7 minutes per side.

Serving Suggestion:

Serve with garlic sauce.

Tip:

Use lean beef.

Bacon Wrapped Asparagus

This is a no-fail recipe that gives you beautiful appetizers each time.

Prep Time and Cooking Time: 15 minutes | Serves: 8

Ingredients to Use:

- 1 lb. asparagus, trimmed
- 6 slices bacon

Step-by-Step Directions

1. Wrap a couple of asparagus with bacon slices.
2. Arrange in a single layer in the air crisper tray.
3. Set your air fryer oven to air fry.
4. Cook at 380 degrees F for 10 minutes.

Tip:

You can also drizzle with maple syrup before air frying.

Italian Olives

Your friends who love olives will definitely enjoy this appetizer.

Prep Time and Cooking Time: 15 minutes | Serves: 8

Ingredients to Use:

- 2 cups green olives, pitted
- 2 cups black olives, pitted
- 2 tablespoons olive oil
- 2 cloves garlic, minced
- ½ teaspoon dried fennel seeds
- ½ teaspoon dried oregano
- Pinch red pepper flakes
- Salt and pepper to taste

Step-by-Step Directions

1. Toss all the ingredients in a bowl.
2. Mix well.
3. Spread the olives in the air crisper tray.
4. Choose air fry setting.
5. Set temperature to 300 degrees F.
6. Cook for 5 minutes.

Serving Suggestion:

Serve immediately.

Tip:

You can also use garlic powder instead of minced garlic.

Mini Lemon Crab Cakes

These are miniature crab cakes that you can serve as appetizer in your next gathering.

Prep Time and Cooking Time: 45 minutes | Serves: 12

Ingredients to Use:

- 24 oz. crab meat
- 3 green onions, chopped
- 3 tablespoons lemon juice
- 3 teaspoons lemon zest
- 6 tablespoons breadcrumbs
- 6 tablespoons mayonnaise

Step-by-Step Directions

1. Combine all the ingredients in a bowl.
2. Shape into 24 small patties.
3. Refrigerate for 30 minutes.
4. Add the mini crab cakes to the air crisper

tray.
5. Set your air fryer oven to air fry.
6. Cook at 370 degrees F for 5 minutes per side or until golden and crispy.

Serving Suggestion:

Garnish with half lemon slices.

Tip:

You can also add fish flakes to the mixture.

Bacon Wrapped Dates

Bacon surely makes everything taste better including dates!
Prep Time and Cooking Time: 15 | Serves: 12

Ingredients to Use:

- 12 slices bacon
- 24 dates, pitted

Step-by-Step Directions

1. Slice the bacon in half.
2. Wrap each date with a bacon slice.
3. Arrange in a single layer in the air crisper tray.
4. Choose air fry setting.
5. Cook at 400 degrees F for 7 to 8 minutes.

Serving Suggestion:

Insert toothpick before serving.

Tip:

You can also dip in balsamic vinegar before air frying.

Bruschetta

This is a simple and easy to prepare appetizer that you'd enjoy serving to your friends.
Prep Time and Cooking Time: 20 minutes | Serves: 12

Ingredients to Use:

- 4 tomatoes, chopped
- 1/4 cup fresh basil leaves, diced
- 1/4 cup Parmesan cheese, shredded
- 1 clove garlic, minced
- 1 tablespoon balsamic vinegar
- 1 teaspoon olive oil
- Salt and pepper to taste
- 1 loaf French bread, sliced
- Cooking spray

Step-by-Step Directions

1. In a bowl, combine all the ingredients except French bread.
2. Top the bread slices with the mixture.
3. Spray the bread with oil.
4. Arrange in a single layer in the air crisper tray.
5. Choose toast or air fry setting.
6. Cook at 250 degrees F for 2 to 3 minutes.

Serving Suggestion:

Sprinkle with pepper.

Tip:

You can also use Italian bread for this recipe.

Pita Chips

These pita chips are versatile and can be paired with most dips.
Prep Time and Cooking Time: 10 minutes | Serves: 8

Ingredients to Use:

- 6 pita breads
- 4 tablespoons olive oil
- 2 teaspoons dried oregano
- Pinch salt

Step-by-Step Directions

1. Slice pita bread into wedges.
2. Brush each side with olive oil.
3. Sprinkle with oregano and salt.
4. Arrange in a single layer in the air crisper tray.
5. Set your air fryer oven to air fry.
6. Cook at 350 degrees F for 1 to 2 minutes

per side.

Serving Suggestion:

Serve with ranch dip or French onion dip.

Tip:

You can also season pita chips with Italian herbs.

Bacon-Wrapped with Scallops

Wrap your scallops with bacon and you have appetizers that will surely impress everyone.
Prep Time and Cooking Time: 30 minutes |
Serves: 4

Ingredients to Use:

- 16 scallops
- 8 slices bacon
- Salt and pepper to taste
- Cooking spray

Step-by-Step Directions

1. Pat scallops dry with paper towel.
2. Slice bacon in half.
3. Wrap scallops with bacon.
4. Secure with toothpick.
5. Spray with oil.
6. Transfer to the air crisper tray.
7. Set the air fryer oven to air fry.
8. Cook at 370 degrees F for 5 minutes per side.

Serving Suggestion:

Drizzle with honey.

Tip:

You can also use turkey bacon to reduce fat and calorie content.

Toasted Caprese Salad

Here's a different take on the famous Italian appetizer.
Prep Time and Cooking Time: 10 | Serves: 6

Ingredients to Use:

- 2 ripe tomatoes, sliced into rounds
- 16 oz. fresh mozzarella cheese, sliced into rounds
- Basil leaves
- 2 tablespoons olive oil
- 3 teaspoons balsamic vinegar
- Pinch Italian seasoning
- Salt and pepper to taste

Step-by-Step Directions

1. Alternate the tomato, mozzarella and basil leaves in a baking pan.
2. Mix oil and vinegar.
3. Drizzle mixture on top of the appetizer.
4. Season with Italian herbs, salt and pepper.
5. Place inside the air fryer oven.
6. Select toast setting.
7. Cook at 320 degrees F for 2 minutes.

Serving Suggestion:

Garnish with herbs.

Tip:

Serve immediately.

Spanakopita

This is a well-known Greek appetizer that you'd surely love.
Prep Time and Cooking Time: 20 minutes|
Serves: 4

Ingredients to Use:

- 2 eggs, beaten
- 10 oz. spinach, chopped
- 4 oz. feta cheese
- Salt and pepper to taste
- 8 mini phyllo shells

Step-by-Step Directions

1. Combine all the ingredients except phyllo shells in a bowl.
2. Top the shells with the mixture.
3. Place the shells inside the air fryer oven.

4. Set it to air fry.
5. Cook at 220 degrees F for 3 minutes.

Serving Suggestion:

Sprinkle with pepper and serve.

Tip:

You can also use frozen spinach for this recipe but thaw first.

Mac & Cheese Balls

Here's a good way to make use of leftover mac and cheese from last night's dinner.

Prep Time and Cooking Time: 30 minutes | Serves: 12

Ingredients to Use:

- 4 cups mac and cheese
- 1 egg, beaten
- 1-1/2 cups breadcrumbs
- 1 tablespoon milk
- Cooking spray

Step-by-Step Directions

1. Combine mac and cheese, egg, breadcrumbs and milk in a bowl.
2. Shape into 24 balls.
3. Spray with oil.
4. Place the balls in the air crisper tray.
5. Set the air fryer oven to air fry.
6. Cook at 350 degrees F for 5 to 7 minutes per side or until golden and crispy.

Serving Suggestion:

Serve with honey mustard sauce.

Tip:

Refrigerate for 1 hour before serving.

Pizza Egg Rolls

These pizza egg rolls explode with so much flavor with each bite.

Prep Time and Cooking Time: 20 minutes | Serves: 12

Ingredients to Use:

- 1 cup pizza sauce
- 24 egg wrappers
- 24 cubes mozzarella cheese
- Italian herbs

Step-by-Step Directions

1. Spread pizza sauce on top of the egg wrappers.
2. Top with the mozzarella cheese.
3. Sprinkle with herbs.
4. Roll or fold the wrapper and seal.
5. Place in the air crisper tray.
6. Choose air fry setting.
7. Cook at 380 degrees F for 10 minutes, flipping once.

Serving Suggestion:

Let cool for 15 minutes before serving.

Tip:

You can also add pepperoni or crumbled sausage to the filling.

Spinach Dip

Use this recipe to prepare this simple but flavorful spinach dip.

Prep Time and Cooking Time: 1 hour | Serves: 12

Ingredients to Use:

- 8 oz. cream cheese, softened
- 1/2 cup onion, minced
- 1/4 teaspoon garlic powder
- 1 cup spinach
- 1 cup mayonnaise
- 1 cup Parmesan cheese, grated
- 1/4 cup water chestnuts , drained and chopped
- Pepper to taste

Step-by-Step Directions

1. Combine all the ingredients in a baking

pan.
2. Mix well.
3. Place the baking pan inside the air fryer oven.
4. Set the air fryer oven to bake.
5. Bake at 300 degrees F for 30 minutes.
6. Stir and cook for another 20 minutes or until edges turn golden.

Serving Suggestion:

Serve with crackers or chips.

Tip:

If using frozen spinach, thaw first before mixing.

Lasagna Egg Rolls

Transform your favorite lasagna into egg rolls with this recipe.
Prep Time and Cooking Time: 45 | Serves: 8

Ingredients to Use:

- 3 cups lasagna noodles, cooked, cooled and diced
- 1/2 cup Italian pasta sauce
- 1/4 cup lean ground beef, cooked
- 1 cup mozzarella cheese, shredded
- 16 egg roll wrappers
- Cooking spray

Step-by-Step Directions

1. In a bowl, mix lasagna noodles, pasta sauce, ground beef and cheese.
2. Top the wrappers with the mixture.
3. Roll up and seal.
4. Spray with oil.
5. Arrange the rolls in the air crisper tray.
6. Set the air fryer oven to air fry.
7. Cook at 380 degrees F for 6 to 8 minutes.

Serving Suggestion:

Serve with marinara dipping sauce.

Tip:

You can also use leftover lasagne for this recipe.

Scotch Eggs

Scotch eggs are delicious and filling appetizer that would surely be a hit in your next get together.
Prep Time and Cooking Time: 30 minutes | Serves: 6

Ingredients to Use:

- 1 lb. bulk sausage, crumbled
- 1 onion, chopped
- 1 teaspoon garlic powder
- 6 hard boiled eggs, peeled
- 1 egg, beaten
- 1 cup coconut flour
- Cooking spray

Step-by-Step Directions

1. Combine sausage, onion and garlic powder in a bowl.
2. Mix well.
3. Form patties from the mixture.
4. Wrap the eggs with this mixture.
5. Dip the Scotch eggs in egg and coat with coconut flour.
6. Spray with oil.
7. Add to the air crisper tray.
8. Set the air fryer oven to air fry.
9. Cook at 400 degrees F for 8 to 10 minutes per side or until golden.

Serving Suggestion:

Serve with hot sauce or mustard.

Tip:

You can also use almond flour.

Green Chili Biscuits

Expect everyone to be impressed with this incredibly simple but delicious appetizer recipe.

Prep Time and Cooking Time: 20 minutes | Serves: 10

Ingredients to Use:

- 2 cups all purpose flour
- 1 teaspoon sugar
- 1 tablespoon baking powder
- 1 teaspoon baking soda
- 1/2 cup butter, melted
- 1/2 cup green chili, chopped
- 1-1/4 cup sour cream
- 1/4 cup cheddar, shredded
- Salt to taste
- Cooking spray

Step-by-Step Directions

1. Combine all the ingredients in a bowl.
2. Mix well.
3. Shape into 20 balls or more.
4. Spray the balls with oil.
5. Place the balls in the air crisper tray.
6. Select bake function.
7. Bake at 340 degrees F for 10 minutes, turning once.

Serving Suggestion:

Serve with garlic butter dip.

Tip:

Use low-fat sour cream.

Sausage & Pineapple Bites

These are some of the simplest yet enticing appetizers recipes you'll ever try.
Prep Time and Cooking Time: 30 minutes | Serves: 10

Ingredients to Use:

- 14 oz. kielbasa sausage, sliced
- 20 oz. pineapple chunks

Step-by-Step Directions

1. Place a pineapple slice on top of the sausage.
2. Insert a toothpick to attach together.
3. Place in the air fryer oven.
4. Set it to grill.
5. Cook at 350 degrees F for 5 minutes.

Serving Suggestion:

Serve with barbecue sauce.

Tip:

You can use either fresh or canned pineapple.

Shrimp & Chorizo Appetizer

Everyone will look forward to your parties when you serve appetizers like this.
Prep Time and Cooking Time: 20 | Serves: 12

Ingredients to Use:

- 24 medium shrimp, peeled and deveined
- 6 links chorizo, sliced into 4 rounds each

Step-by-Step Directions

1. Thread a toothpick through shrimp and chorizo.
2. Add these to the air crisper tray.
3. Select air fry setting.
4. Cook at 370 degrees F for 5 minutes per side.

Serving Suggestion:

Serve in shot glasses with marinara sauce. Garnish with chopped parsley.

Tip:

Cook in batches.

Crunchy Deviled Eggs

Here's a unique twist to the popular deviled eggs appetizer.
Prep Time and Cooking Time: 30 | Serves: 6

Ingredients to Use:

- 6 hard boiled eggs, peeled and sliced in half

- 1 tablespoon yellow mustard
- 1 teaspoon chili powder
- 2 tablespoons mayonnaise
- Salt and pepper to taste
- 3/4 cup all-purpose flour
- 1 egg, beaten
- 1 teaspoon hot pepper sauce
- 1-1/2 cups breadcrumbs
- Cooking spray

Step-by-Step Directions

1. Scoop out the yolks.
2. Add yolks to a bowl.
3. Stir in mustard, chili powder, mayo, salt and pepper.
4. Mash the mixture using a fork. Set aside.
5. Coat the egg white shells with flour.
6. Dip in egg mixed with hot sauce.
7. Dredge with breadcrumbs.
8. Spray with oil.
9. Place these in the air fryer oven.
10. Select air fry function.
11. Cook at 400 degrees F for 3 to 5 minutes per side or until golden.
12. Top with a dollop of egg yolk mixture and serve.

Serving Suggestion:

Sprinkle chopped parsley or green onion on top.

Tip:

You can also skip the chili powder and hot sauce if you don't like your appetizer spicy.

Crostini Tuna Melt Appetizer

These are delicious but easy to prepare appetizer that you won't regret serving to your special guests.
Prep Time and Cooking Time: 10 minutes | Serves: 8

Ingredients to Use:

- 1 French bread loaf, sliced
- 7 oz. canned tuna flakes in oil
- 3/4 cup Parmesan cheese, shaved

Step-by-Step Directions

1. Top the bread slices with tuna flakes and Parmesan cheese.
2. Arrange the bread slices inside the air fryer oven.
3. Select toast setting.
4. Cook at 350 degrees F for 5 minutes.

Serving Suggestion:

Garnish with paprika and fresh dill.

Tip:

You can also use mozzarella cheese for this recipe.

Bacon, Garlic & Cheese Crostini

Expect these appetizers to be gone within a few seconds of serving. They're that good.
Prep Time and Cooking Time: 10 minutes | Serves: 8

Ingredients to Use:

- 3 tablespoons mayonnaise
- 4 oz. cream cheese, softened
- 1/4 teaspoon garlic powder
- 1 French baguette, sliced
- 8 slices bacon, cooked crisp and chopped
- 1 cup cheddar cheese, shredded

Step-by-Step Directions

1. Mix mayo, cream cheese and garlic powder in a bowl.
2. Top the baguette slices with mayo mixture.
3. Sprinkle bacon and cheese on top.
4. Place inside the air fryer oven.
5. Select toast or grill setting.
6. Cook at 350 degrees F for 3 minutes.

Serving Suggestion:

Garnish with herbs.

Tip:

You can also use other types of loaf bread for this recipe.

Crab & Cranberry Bites

Crab meat and cranberry jam may seem like an unlikely pair but they actually go well together.

Prep Time and Cooking Time: 15 minutes | Serves: 8

Ingredients to Use:

- 1/4 cup cream cheese
- 1/4 cup crab meat
- 2 tablespoons green onion, chopped
- 16 mini phyllo shells
- 1/2 cup cranberry sauce

Step-by-Step Directions

1. Mix cream cheese, crab meat and green onion in a bowl.
2. Add phyllo shells to a muffin pan.
3. Top with crab mixture.
4. Place in the air fryer oven.
5. Choose air fry setting.
6. Cook at 370 degrees F for 5 minutes.
7. Top with the cranberry sauce.

Serving Suggestion:

Let cool for 5 minutes before serving.

Tip:

You can also use wonton wrappers for this recipe.

Apple & Goat Cheese Crostini Appetizer

Crunchy, creamy and full of flavor—it's hard to find fault in this wonderful appetizer.

Prep Time and Cooking Time: 10 minutes | Serves: 8

Ingredients to Use:

- 4 oz. goat cheese, crumbled
- 1 tablespoon lemon juice
- 1 teaspoon lemon zest
- 1 French bread, sliced
- 1 apple, sliced thinly

Step-by-Step Directions

1. Mix goat cheese, lemon juice and lemon zest in a bowl.
2. Spread this mixture on top of bread slices.
3. Top with apples.
4. Set inside the air fryer oven.
5. Choose toast function.
6. Cook at 350 degrees F for 5 minutes.

Serving Suggestion:

Garnish with fresh thyme.

Tip:

Use Granny Smith apple if available.

Roasted Sweet Potato Appetizer

This is the kind of appetizer that will impress even the most discerning guests.

Prep Time and Cooking Time: 20 | Serves: 6

Ingredients to Use:

- 3 sweet potatoes, sliced thickly
- 2 tablespoons olive oil
- 1 teaspoon Italian herbs
- 4 oz. feta cheese, crumbled
- 3 tablespoons Greek yogurt

Step-by-Step Directions

1. Toss the sweet potatoes in olive oil.
2. Transfer to the air fryer oven.
3. Select roast setting.
4. Cook at 390 degrees F for 5 minutes per side.
5. Arrange roasted sweet potatoes on a

serving platter.
6. Mix cheese and yogurt.
7. Top sweet potatoes with yogurt mixture and serve.

Serving Suggestion:

Sprinkle with Italian herbs before serving.

Tip:

Use low-fat plain yogurt.

Chili Lime Shrimp Appetizer

This appetizer is not only full of color but also with enticing flavors.
Prep Time and Cooking Time: 15 minutes | Serves: 12

Ingredients to Use:

- 1/2 cup guacamole
- Round tortilla chips
- 1 cup shrimp, cooked
- 1/2 red onion, minced
- 1/2 cup corn kernels
- 1 cup tomatoes, chopped

Dressing

- 2 tablespoons avocado oil
- 3 tablespoons lime juice
- 1 teaspoon garlic powder
- 1 teaspoon onion powder
- 3 teaspoons chili powder
- Salt to taste

Step-by-Step Directions

1. Spread guacamole on top of tortilla chips.
2. Top with shrimp, onion, corn and tomatoes.
3. Mix the dressing ingredients in a bowl.
4. Pour dressing on top of the shrimp mixture.
5. Place inside the air fryer oven.
6. Choose toast setting.
7. Cook at 350 degrees F for 3 minutes.

Serving Suggestion:

Garnish with cilantro.

Tip:

Thaw first if using frozen cooked shrimp or corn kernels.

Sweet & Spicy Sausage Bites

These are incredible appetizers that only take a few minutes of your time.
Prep Time and Cooking Time: 15 minutes | Serves: 8

Ingredients to Use:

- 8 Italian sausage links, sliced into rounds
- 1 cup barbecue sauce
- 2 tablespoons hot pepper sauce
- 1 tablespoon honey

Step-by-Step Directions

1. Mix barbecue sauce, hot pepper sauce and honey in a bowl.
2. Toss sausage slices in the sauce.
3. Insert toothpicks.
4. Place inside the air fryer oven.
5. Choose bake setting.
6. Bake at 370 degrees F for 7 to 10 minutes.

Serving Suggestion:

Serve with mustard.

Tip:

You can also use kielbasa for this recipe.

Conclusion

The basic purpose of this book is to provide a complete guide with recipes to a new appliance called the Breville BOV900BSS Smart Oven Air Convection and Air Fry Countertop Oven.

Once you buy and use this new appliance, you will be impressed with its effectiveness and usefulness as it can do a lot in a limited period of time.

There is no doubt that it is a must-have gadget in the kitchen. In using it for various cooking purposes, you will surely be satisfied with its performance.

It enhances the cooking experience of the user because of its preset mode and rapid heating technology.

Users can take full advantage of the different settings. The recipe locks its nutrients inside the meal. We highly recommend looking into this.

CPSIA information can be obtained
at www.ICGtesting.com
Printed in the USA
BVHW051146111121
621196BV00006B/225